NOTHING HAPPENED

An American Situationist Memoir

By **Isaac Cronin**

Designed and illustrated by **Tanner Goldbeck**

Copyright © 2021 Isaac Cronin, Tanner Goldbeck
All rights reserved.

ISBN 978-0-578-30739-8

One

I grew up in the suburbs of Los Angeles. My family moved there right after the war and my father, David, a hardworking doctor then stationed at Randolph Field in San Antonio Texas in the Army Air Corp, decided that the promised land was going to be California for the future of medicine. This wasn't that hard to imagine in 1948. The city was bursting at the seams. He grew up in a very poor Jewish family in New York. My grandfather literally pushed a fruit cart around the Lower East Side. This story, of working really hard and raising a family, is one that many people from that time went through. For my father that would mean public university in New York, then somehow getting through medical school.

While my father was an incredibly hard worker, he was also deeply troubled. His father, according to the family history, had abandoned the family on the Lower East Side and fallen in love with another woman and then possibly gone back to Europe, leaving the family alone in the Depression.

My father was forced into a very responsible role early on, and that abandonment, that fatal flaw, was always working away at him. He started with family medicine, then became a radiologist, and was able to quickly build a large practice; but at the same time he was always full of self-doubt. In that era, and today as well, Jews often had this institutionalized form of self-loathing where they would change the family name, which my father did in order to get into medical school, and have plastic surgery, which my father also did. In that era anyone who had a family member who was a doctor or a dentist never paid for medical work. It was called professional courtesy. All over the United States you could get any surgical procedure done this way and not pay for it. We all had nose jobs, the entire family, whether we wanted to or not. We were simply told that we were going to have the procedure, and that was that. My father was also self-medicating with alcohol and barbiturates. He would write prescriptions and his staff would fill them. These substances were not as controlled then as they are today.

Seeing, from a very early age, my father fall victim to a progressive, fatal disease like this really undermined my idea of the American success story. Here was this guy who had managed to pull off that incredible coup—an attractive, interesting wife, a family, a successful medical practice—and still he was eaten alive with self-doubt. And my response to that, I think, was the right one. It was to say my father wasn't simply psychologically or emotionally messed up, but rather he wasn't satisfied with what the world was offering him. Something was missing. He was a smart guy; a well-read, cosmopolitan, liberal Jew who was supposed to be happy with everything that he had earned. This was success. Most of his doctor friends who were Jewish were seemingly happy, and they couldn't understand what was going on with him. He had completely abandoned his religion, didn't believe in it. He never made me get a Bar Mitzvah. He was a secular Jew, so he was totally uninterested in having me go to synagogue, or in going to synagogue himself. A lot of people thought that was part of his undoing, that he had abandoned his religious roots for this more atypical approach.

My father was totally in love with Hollywood and movie stars. One way this manifested itself was that when he was looking for a drinking partner in Los

no place like home

Angeles, he found the most notorious drunk in Hollywood at the time to be his bar buddy: Lee Marvin. Marvin was a guy who would close a set for three weeks while on a drunken binge. My father went on many trips to Mexico with him, and who knows what they did down there? I don't want to know. This really undermined my sense of the traditional society, the traditional family, the American dream, the big payoff, happiness at the end of the rainbow, and all the rest of it. I saw that this wasn't going to work.

Another institution that dissolved before my eyes was psychiatry. My father passed away from his bad habits in 1963, when I was fifteen. At that time, I was seeing a psychiatrist whose name was Richard Lieberman. I remember that he was so ugly, he looked like a frog; he was just hideous, and I hated going there. One day he called my mother and me in, and he said to her, "Your son really is doing incredibly well." I was thinking, "Oh, really? My father just died two months ago and I'm okay?" I didn't want to go anyway, so it was actually fine with me. But then he added, "I really think if Isaac is going to continue to see me, he should pay for the treatment himself." And my mother looked at him like, "What? He's fifteen. He's in his last year of high school. We don't need him to work for the money for him to pay you." He was trying to get rid of us, and my suspicion is he was basically saying, "I'm throwing you out because I really don't want to be involved in a Jewish professional family where the head of the household overdoses. I don't want anything to do with this." It was really another abandonment by the medical profession, first by my father and then by Lieberman. I was thinking, "I really don't want to be in this line of work."

Right after my father died, my mother was also seeing a psychiatrist and when she, not surprisingly, had a breakdown, she was sent into a mental health sanitarium. When she got there, her psychiatrist tried to have sex with her, and she fled back home. Within just a few months, this whole thing, this enterprise of psychiatry, crumbled for me really. These are all building blocks of that world, and little bits and pieces of it were crumbling one by one.

At the same time all this was happening I was looking for a positive vision of some kind. I had a group of friends who were as bohemian as you could get in the LA/San Fernando Valley of 1963–64, and we were looking for an alternative. The pop music scene had just begun to change with the Beatles, the Byrds, and others. But we were all about being outsiders, so what were we going to glom onto? Jazz, that was our world. My father had actually introduced me to that music because growing up in New York he listened to Duke Ellington and Count Basie. When I was younger, he played Ray Charles records. He was on the liberal side of all that, even in the early sixties.

My friends and I created a world based on jazz. We had a group of four or five of us, who would go to the Lighthouse, a club in Hermosa Beach where all the great jazz players at the time would perform, as there were still a lot of them alive. We would go to the Topanga Mall, one of the first malls in Los Angeles, and sit in these glass booths at Wallachs Music City, where they would let you break out new albums and listen to them. We would play these jazz records, and as we were listening, there would be this procession of what we would call "Normals," the suburban people, walking by. We had a whole definition of "us" as opposed to "them." This was our identity back then. I think in a way it was very snotty and crass, but it was also positive. Norman Mailer a few years later wrote an essay called "The White Negro" that dealt with some of these ideas. We didn't copy the African-American slang exactly, or maybe a little bit, but we weren't literally trying to be like the "wiggers," the term then for white kids who sought to emulate black culture. We were just trying to find an interesting alternative world. And that was it for us—that was the positive in this sea of the negative.

My father died in August of 1963 at the age of forty-six, very young. Three months later, also at the age of forty-six, John Kennedy was killed, a coincidence that affected me profoundly. We were all still in mourning for my father, while at that same moment we were watching the funeral for Kennedy on television, and at that moment my father's passing, my personal tragedy, and the death of the father of the country were fused in my adolescent mind, an amalgam of the personal and the political, a sense that everything that was going on at home was mirrored in the society.

Boredom had always been a really powerful force in my life. Msupposedly ideal childhood had obviously been interrupted by a lot of things, but in terms of affluence, privilege and possibility it was still all very ideal, at least on the surface. Yet I found it all excruciatingly boring. I was overwhelmed by that. Years later I did a video about the poverty of modern life, Call It Sleep. I remember walking by the family book collection, which was pretty large, and there was a book that I always stopped in front of. It was Call It Sleep, by Henry Roth, which was a semi-autobiographical novel about growing up in the Jewish ghetto in the Lower East Side during the beginning of the 20th Century. I didn't even really know what was in the book. I just loved the title, because everything I did was about being bored and trying to escape boredom, a kind of "sleep." I didn't really locate the source of that boredom then as precisely as I do now. It was all about this undifferentiated suburban life that I found excruciatingly tedious, and that I would do anything to escape.

Like rock musicians later in the sixties, many of our jazz heroes died really young, even if they didn't die of drugs. I loved the guitarist Wes Montgomery, who died at forty-five. John Coltrane, Charlie Parker, Lee Morgan, Art Pepper, Eric Dolphy, Chet Baker. We know the stories. Recently I was looking back at my high school friends who were in the group with me, just to see what happened to them. One died of an overdose in his thirties, and the other one, who was my closest friend, his girlfriend murdered him when he was sixty years old. In a way, I didn't realize it, but I was a survivor of all this.

My interest in psychiatry hadn't really stopped. I went to college at UC Berkeley in 1964, and I had to declare my major in something to get a liberal arts degree. I decided I was going to be a psychologist. Being one of these kids who was engaged by the real world and always wanting to try things out, in the summer of '65 I decided I was going to get a job, a self-appointed internship at the local VA hospital in Sepulveda in the San Fernando Valley, a few miles from my mother's home. I lied about my age as I was seventeen and you had to be eighteen to work for the federal government. I had already finished my first year at Berkeley, so I went in there and basically said, I'm through with Berkeley and my academic career. I really want to be an orderly, a bedpan slinger, government service 2, which is the lowest paying job. That was pretty bold. They gave me a test, and the head instructor was like Nurse Ratched from One Flew Over the Cuckoo's Nest. Her name was O'Grady. She said, "You really want to do this?" And I said, "Yeah, I really want to try this out. Maybe I'll go back to school someday, but for now this seems okay." They hired me, and there was an eight-week orientation where I learned how to empty a bedpan, change sheets, and make a bed with perfect hospital corners. The rest of the training was half-medical and half-psychiatric.

The first day, I remember, I walked onto the ward wearing those starched whites, with the big metal keys jangling from my chain, and all the other workers with me were African-American, from South Central LA—a low-income black neighborhood in the city. I was the only guy under thirty and the only white person in that job. And there we were on a ward filled with veterans suffering from combat fatigue, or PTSD (Post Traumatic Stress Disorder) as it's now called,

victims from World War II and the Korean War. They were "shell-shocked," and they had no idea what was really going on. The patients from World War II were in their forties, and the ones from the Korean War were in their thirties, and they were all there in these locked wards. There was a battered black-and-white TV in the dayroom tuned to soap operas all the time. There were patients walking around mumbling. They had just introduced a powerful drug called Thorazine, the first of a new generation of really powerful antipsychotics. What it did was while the patient kept on hallucinating auditorily and visually, they didn't get so freaked out by what they were seeing and hearing because they were so sedated. They called it liquid shock therapy, and they would give doses that were eight to ten times what they give now for these diagnoses. Many patients would gain weight, despite the fact that the second biggest drug on the ward was cigarettes. They really wanted these guys to smoke. They had a duty-free, tax-free, store for that. It was a commissary, like on an army base. I remember the cigarettes were a dollar a carton, ten cents a pack. Outside they were twenty-five cents, but here they were ten. These guys would smoke three, four or five packs a day, and they would get yellow fingers from nicotine, but they would still walk around slowly.

  As part of our education they took us to see an ECT (Electrical Convulsive Therapy) session. We walked in and there was a guy on a gurney, and they gave him a shot to knock him out and he was restrained. Back then for ECT sessions they used huge doses of electricity that were really convulsive. The goal was to scramble your brain, essentially, and they never knew how or why it worked. It was a last resort. They turned on the electricity, and this guy started convulsing. I just fainted away. I've never fainted before or after. I woke up in the hallway, and O'Grady said, "There's always one who passes out." What I learned though from this, before the Vietnam War really revved up and got going, was that this is the outcome of war. This was my first realization, the first step for me, in the unraveling of the official explanation of what war was about, seeing these veterans and their suffering.

One of the most common delusions for people who've been in combat is that they think they're Napoleon. Literally there was more than one Napoleon on our ward. Two patients would fight for who would get to be Napoleon. They would have this existential moment and they had to figure out who got to be Napoleon that day. What I concluded is that these people knew that they were cannon fodder. To be Napoleon is to be the one who decides, the one who gets to actually make the decisions, the one who turns the cannon fodder machine on, who turns people into bodies. I think that makes sense in a way. If you're going to be somebody powerful, as a delusion of grandeur, you're going to be the general; it could be Eisenhower, or somebody else, but somehow Napoleon is a more glamorous figure in this process.

The second month of working at the VA the Watts Riots happened. It was the second week of August 1965. South Central LA is fifteen miles away from the San Fernando Valley over the coastal hills, but the whole city was covered in smoke. This was a week of riots where thousands of buildings were damaged, where whole blocks were set on fire and where many people were killed and wounded by police and National Guard gunfire. It was the biggest insurrection of the civil rights era. James, my dapper coworker, who had a red conk hairstyle and loved jazz—that gave us a common language—approached me at lunch. He had been gone for a week and had called in sick. He said, "I got something to show you." We went over to the parking lot and he opened up his trunk and there was an entire men's haberdashery of stuff that had been looted from the riots. There were records, leather jackets, cognac, just a whole world of stuff. That made sense because the rioters had looted hundreds of stores and they

didn't burn the merchandise. I looked at it all and I thought, "Can I really buy this from him? This is so noble. Bringing money into the equation cheapens what they did." I didn't speak for a few seconds, then I said, "I can't really do this." Then he said, "You really should come down and hang out with us in Watts because we have all these garage sales every weekend. There's washing machines, dryers, stereos, TVs. It's all there for sale." This went on for years actually. This is another side of that period that had an incredibly powerful impact on me.

At that point I identified so closely with the African-American world. In addition to jazz, I used to listen to rhythm and blues in the early sixties. There was Tina Turner, Jackie Wilson, as well as all these great bands, James Brown. They were just entering the white world barely. You had to really dig to find them. You had to know what the soul station was, the jazz station. I became a hero among my friends because my mother, out of guilt, I think, for what happened with my father, bought me a car. She had sold my father's medical practice, and our standard of living declined dramatically after that. We had to sell the house we were living in. She had to go back to work. It all changed very conclusively. But as a kind of transition point into that, she bought a car for me, and I remember it because it had FM radio, which back then was very new. You could listen to the jazz station. My car was the only car that anyone wanted to ride in anywhere because we could listen to jazz on the radio. It just seems incomprehensible now that it would matter so much, but it did. Back then, if you could have that sound of freedom beaming into your car, that was very cool.

With Watts, another pillar of that world collapsed. Alongside the American dream of success and the belief that psychology/psychiatry was a helpful science was the idea that the world was working out for everyone. I totally identified with the guys from South Central. These were the cool people, they were the ones who really understood how to live, how to play music, how to have fun. If these people were rioting, if they weren't being treated properly, I felt that to be an injustice that would affect everybody.

In a way I think my mother was naive and didn't do me any great service, because I had been accelerated in school and skipped some grades when I was younger. At the age of sixteen, I was told it was time to go to college. I think it would have been smart actually for me not to do that. I was thrown into Berkeley. I was ecstatic in a way because I got to leave the suburbs behind, but on the other hand I was in way over my head. I was leaving home for good at the age of sixteen, but carrying all this baggage of someone older. I was cynical, I was unhappy, I was bored. I thought, what could change my perspective? And fortunately, I landed in the most fascinating city in America at its most interesting period.

I was lucky. If I had landed there two years later, at eighteen, the right age for a freshman, it would have been very different. It would have still been interesting, but there wouldn't have been this sea change happening in front of me that was the FSM (Free Speech Movement). That was really fortunate in informing my perspective in many ways. Almost more important than the FSM, though, was what I saw walking down Telegraph Avenue in Berkeley in September of 1964. I'd had a fairly sophisticated upbringing in the suburbs of Los Angeles, which were part of an incredibly racially segregated city, but this was different. I walked down the street, and I remember the very first day seeing a lot of mixed race kids and couples, and I thought, "Wow, this is so cool. You're not in Simi Valley anymore! You're not in Northridge!" It wasn't just racial harmony, it was my idea of the jazz scene come to life on the streets of Berkeley.

There was also this incredible concentration of great bookstores and record stores in Berkeley. The record stores would each only carry one or two categories of music. You had one record store on the corner of Bancroft and Telegraph that only had jazz and classical music—that's all they sold. Another one carried rock and pop music, and so on. I was also reading Downbeat magazine, and I knew about every record when it came out, I knew every artist that was on it. I wasn't collecting as a fetish, but I had a few hundred records, maybe more. I would go in these record stores and talk to these guys behind the counter for hours. And the people who worked in the stores knew everything, and they had amazing sound systems, and it was pouring out onto the street. There were all these record stores and bookstores along with this racially mixed street environment that created something special and wonderful.

There were also a couple of art house cinemas. At that point in 1964 you could not see foreign films anywhere. There were only a couple of dozen theaters in the U.S. that showed them. European films were in their heyday; the cinema from over there was powerful and interesting. And from the rest of the world: Rashomon played in a theater on Telegraph for two or three years straight. It was that kind of town. And then there were the coffeehouses. People were arguing loudly about politics and the issues of the day, in large part because the Free Speech Movement was at its height and encouraged this discourse. At that time you couldn't find espresso coffee in the United States or in the Bay Area except at those coffeehouses, like Mediterraneum and the Forum, and a few in North Beach in San Francisco.

And then there was the Free Speech Movement itself, which was very powerful. It was not simply about the idea of free speech but also a response to the limiting of political discourse. But this was an instance where the Situationists were among the only people to catch on to what the Free Speech Movement was really about. With the FSM, we are talking about a class of people—the technocrats and the future white-collar workers, the future bosses, the future corporate middle-level bureaucrats—and seeing what was going to happen to them. And this aspect of it was really Mario Savio, one of the leaders of the FSM, at his best, rejecting that role to the extent that he could. This made sense to me because I understood from my limited critique of the "Normals" that I really didn't want to do that. I could see that there was going to be more boredom on the way. Sadly, the traditional Left, the whole alphabet soup of traditional leftist groups—the Trotskyists and Bolsheviks and Maoists—saw that militancy, that anger, that unhappiness, that unrest, and turned it into a very channeled, focused critique of the Vietnam War. For me, that wasn't nearly as interesting as the original critique the FSM leaders had made, especially Savio. That was a tragic turn for me.

Going over to San Francisco was very exotic and had its own very special identity. I remember going for the first time at night to North Beach. It seemed like a whole other world. I had been exposed to the Beatniks, I'd read Howl, but their power had been eclipsed. They had been displaced by the Civil Rights Movement and the FSM. Their cultural power had waned.

My mother was still in her guilty mode, so she suggested that I visit my cousin in New York City for the 1965 Christmas holiday. My cousin, Anne, had had a very preppy life. She was four years older than me and very sophisticated as she had gone to a boarding school in New York and had fallen in love with this guy, Simon Roosevelt, the great-grandson of Theodore Roosevelt and the grandson of E. E. Cummings. She had gotten married and joined this very blue blood family. Simon's uncle, Kermit, had planned and executed the coup to overthrow prime minister Mohammad Mosaddegh in Iran in 1953, and Kermit had been a CIA operative; this was a family of the American Empire. Anne married this guy and then immediately got pregnant. He got drunk one night and drove his motorcycle a hundred miles an hour on the West Side Highway, running into a parked police car. He died—they were both twenty. It was another sad story for me. Another way things weren't working out. Everything seems to be going just right, and then, self-destruction. It was building up in me. I didn't identify with John Kennedy personally, but there was just a lot of violence, murder and mayhem going on—exemplified by his assassination—that was undermining what I was supposed to be thinking at that point. There was a violence in the air.

My cousin Anne had inherited the family apartment, a beautiful place in the West Village. I was seventeen and she was twenty-one and widowed. She got a job as the coat check girl at the most glamorous discotheque in New York at the time. It was called Arthur and had been started by Sybil Burton, Richard Burton's ex-wife, whom Richard left to marry Elizabeth Taylor. She started this glamorous nightclub, and somehow my cousin—perhaps because of her golden "Roosevelt" name—got a job as the coat check girl. For two weeks I went there every night. The drinking age in New York was eighteen then, and I was seventeen, so I slid by. I was smoking cigarettes and I thought I was really cool. I would go to this club for free and drink all night. There was only one club to go to in New York really, and everyone who was on the A-list at that time would come to this place: Leonard Bernstein, Truman Capote, Andy Warhol, Sophia Loren, Julie Andrews. They would all dance. It was kind of fun.

I was also seeing how superficial it was to a certain extent. I would sneak out around eleven or twelve and go to jazz clubs like the Village Vanguard, and I really felt at home there. I remember one of my biggest heroes at the time was this white blues singer from Mississippi who had totally figured out how to be black without seeming to be trying to be black. His name was Mose Allison. He did a couple of traditional songs that were big hits, like "Seventh Son," and he had this great boogie-woogie piano style. He also had that kind of voice where you couldn't really tell if he was white or black. He was elegant, and I really identified with him. I thought this is a guy who's figured out how to be in this world as an artist and be radical, but not completely give up his own identity. He was a really strong role model for me.

I'm thinking about my relationship to African-Americans. Given so much proximity and so much going on at that time in difficult circumstances, it made sense that I would gravitate toward that scene as a perpetual subject of interest and that I would feel comfortable moving in and out of that world. For example, I remember that in 1965, when I was on that trip to New York, I saw that James Brown was playing at the Apollo. Being precocious musically, I knew exactly what that meant, and who he was, and how important he was. I went to Harlem and there were only a couple of other white people there, but it was okay because they thought, "if you're here for that, that's cool." I saw James Brown do his whole act with his cape. I think that kind of experience allowed me to be much more comfortable in that world without feeling like I was a tourist, even though I didn't have that upbringing and I didn't have that history. I felt like I had experienced it enough firsthand that it was okay for me, that I didn't have to explain why I was there. I felt like someone who, from another angle, appreciated that experience.

I suffered through all the highs and lows of the sixties, because there were a lot of transcendent moments as well. And those incredible moments always pushed me toward the sense that a community was possible. How to define that was difficult, but a community that was as different as possible from what I was traditionally supposed to experience when I was young in the suburbs. My mother was also raised in a very tolerant, open-minded Jewish liberal household in New York, but she couldn't understand why this turn in her life was not what she deserved. She could never grasp why I would head off in another direction. She never understood why I didn't want to be a doctor. I think I've laid out an incredibly convincing argument for why I wouldn't want to pursue that profession. It was heartless and mercenary and cruel to me personally. I just couldn't bridge that gap.

The bohemian culture, which the Beats overestimated in some sense, was for some of us a bridge, it wasn't an end in itself, to that whole African-American jazz world. But we were encouraged to think that it could be enough to make a superficial rejection of the straight world. When we showed up in Berkeley in 1964, it's hard to get a handle on how uniform and narrow the range of choices were in every cultural and social category. Literally everyone, whether it was an FBI agent or a student or a teacher (am I leaving anybody out?) dressed in the same conservative manner. You could not tell people apart. They were wearing sport coats or blazers and ties. They were wearing slacks and dress oxford shirts. The time of 1964–65 was the moment when people's hair got longer for various reasons. But until that point the range of choices, whether it was in food or music or anything else, was incredibly homogeneous. There were certain ways you could tell a radical. They wore blue jeans, a tweed coat with patches, carried a green book bag and had long sideburns and smoked a pipe, a uniform that was just developing then. Because if you look at what people wore in the Civil Rights Movement, they were totally normally dressed, often in a suit and tie. Though their behavior was not normal, their appearance was indistinguishable from any other person.

Jazz was an acceptable category, but it wasn't fragmented into subgenres then. The British sound was part of pop, it wasn't separate from it. It was all really the same. The whole range of choices in every aspect of life was so narrow. You could sense these people at the top, the decision makers, in that moment come to the realization that they had to expand the choices or risk a revolt based on monotony. They were very collaborative with each other in figuring out a way to provide an almost endless variety that didn't really require true participation. And that was a brilliant move, I think.

It's funny, I guess it was just a factor of my age, but when I first came to Berkeley, I was so young and insecure and trying to figure out the lay of the land. My mother was terrified of what might happen if I lived in my own apartment at the age of seventeen. She wouldn't let me live in an apartment. This was a hilarious transition. I said, "If I can't live in an apartment and I hate the dormitory, what's left?" She said, "Why don't you join a fraternity?" I joined a fraternity. It was a nightmare. It was unbelievable what was going on there because the world was all falling apart and these people were playing bridge, they were totally oblivious to the whole thing. They kicked me out after a semester. I would show up dressed in weird clothes that they hated. They wouldn't let me play the music I loved, so I realized that I had to get out of there.

What made it clear to me that it was time to leave home for good? I had no choice as it turned out. In that era the generational conflict embodied an intense polarization of social perspectives, and it led to a great deal of drama. My mother had found a guy named Murph through a divorced dating group. Murph was so much the opposite of my father in every way— he was a working-class Polish Catholic, a carpenter, a political reactionary who was rigid, vulgar and prone to rage. For him I was the embodiment of my father and of my generation and therefore an enemy to be attacked at every opportunity. By the second summer of that relationship, in 1966, there were constant arguments based on his complaints about my messiness, appearance, selfishness—the usual Archie Bunker bullshit. There was even a little shoving by Murph. For very unclear motives he proposed we take a camping trip to Vancouver Island in British Columbia. The silences were deafening as we rode north on Interstate

5. At one point somewhere in Oregon he turned to me and with a ghoulish sneer said, "You and your father, you think you own the world, but you are both nothing but shit. Your mom told me how miserable your father made her, and she doesn't have anything positive to say about your selfish ass either. Why don't you do the whole family a favor and jump out of the car right now. You won't be missed." He was a miserable monster, but this was something extreme even for this fool. We rode on in silence for hours. Somehow we managed to finish the trip without another outburst. I felt so terrible that I had recommended my mother marry Murph a few months after they met. I felt worse for her, as she had to live with this reptile. When we got home and I told her what he had said, my mother responded with "Oh, he didn't mean that. He does have a temper. I am sure it will be forgotten." I protested, but she was done with the topic. A few weeks later I went back to school and told my mother she should turn my room into a spare bedroom. Murph had made it easy. Imagine how ugly it would have gotten as his world fell apart, and I embodied that process.

Two

I can't emphasize too much the significance of the lived experience of being in those moments. Thirty-six years later I was in New York on 9/11 in Brooklyn a half a mile or so across the river from the tip of Manhattan and the World Trade Center. From the roof of my apartment building I saw the second plane hit the tower and heard the sound of that impact and saw Manhattan disappear. I was moved to immediately start editing a book about terrorism, Confronting Fear, that was published in May of 2002. That's an example of having such a physical, emotional, sensual experience a cataclysmic event that it produced a very physical and psychological reaction in me of wanting to understand what happened. In 1965 the experience of having my friend and coworker at the hospital, James, open up his truck and show me that surprising loot and explain to me in his own words why it was fair that he got that, and having to agree with him—you can't really replace that with any Internet experience you can walk away from.

When I showed up in Berkeley in 1964, aside from going to classes I wandered a lot through the campus, and one of the things I later realized was that, in comparison to today, there really wasn't any way to experience daily life except in the first person. You didn't have any media tools, but I had my eyes open to my own experience. I walked through the courtyard below Sproul Plaza across from Dwinelle Hall, by the fraternity boys. They were called the Freddies, and the sorority girls were called the Sallies. The fraernity boys had a very rigid outfit; they wore the blue button-down or madras plaid dress shirts popularized by the TV show Doby Gillis, starring Dwayne Hickman as a somewhat aimless, coventional teenager sparring with his best friend Maynard G. Krebs (Bob Denver), TV's first beatnik. Again taking off from Dobie, the boys wore white jeans and saddle shoes or penny loafers. They also sat according to a very rigid hierarchy of coolness on the top rung of the benches, never on the seats. The sorority girls were on the other side, like at a high school dance. The girls all wore plaid pleated skirts with cardigan sweaters, kneesocks, and penny loafers.

Through Sather Gate there was a spread of tables and then all of a sudden there was this sea of difference—the sights and sounds of protest. People handing out literature. Speakers with megaphones filling the air with polemics. It was electric. There was no media covering it. Even if you weren't active in the sense that you had made a commitment, you formed your own opinion right there and then, you experienced this viscerally. I was still trying to sort out where I stood at that point.

By 1965 there were already 300,000 troops in Vietnam. You can peg the radicalism of the antiwar movement directly to the size of the troop presence in Asia. It makes sense because the war was coming home, people were dying. In the spring of 1965 I started seeing posters in the Berkeley student union for the Vietnam Day Committee events. The word imperialism was finally showing up outside of Leninist texts and entered the American mainstream. The idea was that there were still colonies where the exploited lived and suffered—it was basic class consciousness. The third world was a term that also came into common use right around that time, partly from Frantz Fanon, the political philosopher who'd written The Wretched of the Earth. The "third world" was presumably the home of the true proletariat, the true oppressed. And so literally, almost overnight, this critique of university life, the daily life of the The Air-Conditioned Nightmare, as the title of Henry Miller's conroversial travelogue called America—all of that critique was put aside. The thrust became "We really are responsible for the people in Vietnam, who are in fact our brothers and sisters overseas, who are suffering in part because we're doing so well here." In effect the concept of guilt was introduced at the same time as paternalism. We could no longer spend time on this other movement that was criticizing basic institutions, but only on the Vietnam War that we were involved in. The critique of the society at large and the university was abandoned.

That approach continued through the end of the New Left and really determined its character. What was unfortunate in some ways was that the abandoned critique of daily life as such was taken on by the counterculture. In other words, it was not totally put aside, it was hijacked. And the result was a roundabout, sweet, gentle, naive critique of daily life that was entered into without much debate. It's almost impossible to overemphasize how deep the antagonism was between the politicos and the hippies, as they had almost nothing in common. They might have shared some drug use, but even the interpretation of drugs and their supposed consequences, as well as usefulness to a critique of society, was not held in common at all. There clearly was an opening because of the exposure of the fake optimism of the first twenty years after World War II, the forced consumption that was required in a consumer society, and the uniformity of daily life, especially in the suburbs. At that point it was pretty much intolerable and couldn't go on uncontested.

The hippie approach was: We don't really like what's going on so we have come up with a better vision, a more human, playful, interesting way to live. They thought the old world of capitalism would just wither away and die. There was a brief period in which there was a dual power situation in the youth movement. Calling somebody a hippie, even by 1967, was generally seen as an insult. If you were a radical, you held in great contempt the idea that you would passively accept most of what was going on in the world in order to create a utopian alternative.

We lived in this bubble, which was even more insular than the bicoastal world of today. I drove across the country a couple of times, but my life was in the Bay Area of San Francisco and in New York. The rest of the country didn't even exist for us. Thinking back today, it was a great era for costumes. If you were a hippie, part of your wardrobe was Native American, part was an Indian ashram outfit, part was Elizabethan English. You were constantly wearing costumes and constantly changing them and remixing them. It was a hysterical, colorful, wild circus atmosphere, especially in contrast to what had come before.

Three

In the Fall of 1966 I moved to UC Santa Cruz from Berkeley, to study Freud, who wasn't taught there at the time. I remember one of the first days that I was in Santa Cruz I decided, along with my friend Ron Berger, who'd come with me, that the way to be really cool and hip, and also radical, was to look, act, and dress like a real worker, that is, like a blue collar worker. Ron was very romantic, and he thought, "What's the meanest, toughest thing you can do to make a living in this town?" It was to be a commercial fisherman. The job was dangerous, dirty, and did not pay well. He decided to get a job and dress like those commercial fishermen, and I went along just for the adventure. Monterey was still an active fishing port, along with Moss Landing. The fisheries had mostly disappeared because of massive overfishing and agricultural toxins that had polluted the area, but they were still catching some squid. I remember walking on campus after having been up all night fishing using nets. In the morning we were wearing blue jeans and work shirts and rubber boots covered with fish scales. The point was to show these spoiled middle-class kids, most of them from upper-middle-class West Los Angeles families, that we were the real deal, part of the sea, the salt of the earth—which we weren't, we were acting. So once again, it was a costume.

As the war escalated, there were 400,000 troops in Vietnam in '67, up to the high point of 550,000 by '68, as the numbers kept getting bigger month by month, and the pressure became more intense. Every guy was feeling the heat. It's impossible today to imagine that your life could be taken over by the state, and that you could die six months after you graduated from college. There are no comparable experiences today, nothing to match this intensity. It was a multidimensional, radicalizing experience because you had this profound existential choice you could not escape.

You started from your role as a spoiled middle-class kid with moral issues about the war you had studied. From reading and listening to the various radical or New Left historians, you didn't want to be part of an occupying army in a third world country. Figuring out your plan became an obsession. There were so many discussions, mostly among men, but with women as well. What were you going to do? Were you going to go to Canada or would you apply for conscientious objector status? Nobody I knew intended to go into the military.

The situation was that if you weren't enrolled in a college at the age of eighteen, you got your induction notice. You went to the induction center in your city of residence to take a one-day physical, and you either passed or failed. If you passed, two months later you were sent for basic training to a base, such as Fort Ord on the Monterey Peninsula. You went through a brief boot camp training period and then you were sent to Vietnam. If you were in school, you got a deferment until you finished your undergraduate degree, or four years elapsed after you had started the college process. There was none of this "taking fewer units and hanging out at school." This was a streamlined conveyor belt to maximize body flow.

One of the great moments of resistance to the war was the attempt to close the military enrollment centers around the United States in the fall of 1967. On the day of the Stop the War protests thousands of people gathered in the streets around Clay Street in Oakland chanting and dodging the cops with their billy clubs. Some chained themselves to the front door of their house. Most of my friends decided that to prove their point they actually wanted to get arrested. Hundreds of people went to the county jail. I didn't. I didn't really want those people to have control over me. The protesters didn't succeed in closing the induction center, but it was one of the memorable events of the Bay Area antiwar movement, and many people who later became leaders in the New Left made their mark by being arrested there, such as Dan Siegel, Frank Bardacke, and others.

The night before the demonstration Ron came over to me at the apartment we shared and put his arm around my shoulder. He looked at me intensely, as this was clearly a heavy moment. He told me Suebi, his girlfriend, didn't want him to do anything the next day that would separate all of us, but if it happened, they had agreed that I could stay in their bed, and if I wanted to sleep with Suebi, Ron was fine with that. Did I need any more encouragement? Ron spent a month in jail, and Suebi and I did enjoy each other.

There was a movement called the Resistance, started by David Harris, who later married Joan Baez. She was everywhere, giving speeches, demonstrating. Baez was the fantasy girlfriend of many male activists. She was beautiful, long-haired, she had an amazing voice, and she was passionate. She and Harris often came to Santa Cruz, and of course everyone was with them. They didn't really have to recruit men to symbolically burn their draft cards, which didn't really mean very much, because you didn't really need your draft card. The Selective Service had your number and knew where to find you. I got my induction notice after I graduated from UCSC in June of 1968. They picked you up in Santa Cruz. This was the worst bus ride of my life. There were sixty people on the bus, and all of them going to take their induction physicals. Wow. This was like Take the Money and Run, the Woody Allen movie that has the bus ride to the Southern chain gang. It was really grim.

In my world, there were certain options not available to all. There were certain doctors who were totally against the war and they would help you dodge it. They wouldn't take any money; they refused to accept a penny. There was one in Palo Alto, a very kind guy, who said to me, "I do not want you to go to the war, so I will write you a letter, but only if you tell me something that's really wrong with you and I'll exaggerate it. I won't make up something out of nothing. That's just too much." I thought that since I'd been fishing I had developed a slightly bad back. I had back pain because I was pulling in the nets. He said, "That's good, that makes sense. But we need to make it a little worse. So I think you have to have a slipped disk because a slipped disc doesn't show on an X-ray. I have a colleague at Stanford Hospital who is one of the top orthopedic guys in the United States, and he'll write you a letter too." I had a portfolio of letters and I had a back brace. I was a mess for that day.

Entering the induction center was bedlam. The place was insane and very loud. People were acting out, doing everything. Some would take their clothes off. Some were yelling, "I love the Vietcong. I want them to win!" Traitorous statements. There were some amazing stories. One of my friends who was this kind of Marlboro man who spoke with a Texas drawl, said, "What do you think about this? What if I say the same sentence over and over again without stopping for ten hours, you think it will work?" And I said, "Well, I don't know, what are you going to say?" He said, "What about 'I'm an old cowpoke, but I don't smoke.'" He did exactly that, and after five hours of it the supervising sergeant threw him out. Wow. That was pretty brilliant. That Texan saved his own life as far as I'm concerned.

Another interesting story involved Paul Mann, who later became an important member of the Situationist group we started in Berkeley in 1970.

He discovered that the draft board had a requirement related to minimum and maximum weight for each person's height. Over or under and you got an automatic deferment. Paul was very skinny, and if you were six-foot-three like him and weighed under 135 pounds, which is emaciated, you got a deferment. He decided to try and lose the ten or fifteen pounds he needed to. For a month he didn't eat, and for the first four days we all fasted with him. There were six of us, and two of us took him to the induction center to give him a send-off. But when he came back from his physical, he couldn't walk he was so weak. He got his 1Y.

My deferment for a slipped disk came, and it was also 1Y, which, unlike 4F, meant they could have called me again in a national emergency. I don't know if I would call it privilege, but I was fortunate to be in a very intelligent environment that allowed me to have this option. And I know there are plenty of people who, if they'd have had this opportunity, they would have taken it.

At the high point of the antwar movement, there were demonstrations growing exponentially across the country, including the march on the Pentagon with a half a million people. Our radical group at UCSC didn't really want to participate in those protests because we thought we would get lost in the crowd. The world sees 1968 as the great moment of youthful revolt, the high point of radical activity post–World War II. There were uprisings in many countries besides the U.S., especially France and Germany. Hundreds, if not thousands, of people were killed in protests in Mexico that year. America's moment was at the Democratic Convention in Chicago in 1968, but a lot was going on all over the world. The biggest revolt for many of us on the Left that year was May/June in Paris, because that was the one time when there really did seem to be an alliance between the students, the intellectuals, and the workers. It's worth noting that we did not find out about how radical and groundbreaking the French movement was until 1969. None of us watched the news on TV; I didn't even know anyone with a TV set. There was no alternative other than talking to people who had been there or reading books or magazine articles in the mainstream weeklies, which were totally baffled by the critique of daily life that was manifesting in the streets. In a way there was no context even for us to understand what happened until we were able to read the works of the Situationists.

The other influence that was really important in 1967–68 was the Black Panthers. You can't leave that out in the Bay Area. No matter what you think about them, they had a huge presence. They were very powerful, very charismatic, and even people like me and my comrades, who were already embracing a libertarian critique of society, had to admire their courage in terms of confronting the police and mobilizing a lot of people.

Once again, the costume was important. You didn't have to really look like Che Guevera, you didn't have to wear camo, the jungle suit, the Cuban revolutionary outfit. The Panthers came up with a new look, this urban guerrilla outfit where you could have the great black leather coat, the blue turtleneck, the combat boots, and the beret, and they pulled it off. I don't mean to diminish it, but I do think these things are important. The theatricality of it was a great draw for people. The attitude and the guns helped, but the look was really important. And so as sheepish as we were about participating in Panther-related events, because we knew in terms of the actual content of what they were saying it was completely reformist and not the sort of radical political program we were after, we went along briefly. They wanted soup kitchens and afterschool programs; we wanted to change society. I remember going to a demonstration at the Federal Building in San Francisco when Huey Newton, a senior member of the Black Panther Party, was in jail, and yelling along with several thousand other people,

"Free Huey or the sky's the limit!" And I turned to someone and said, "Do we know what that means? The sky's the limit, but what does that really mean? What's going to happen? What are we really going to do if they don't free him?"

It was a hustle. Most activism is of course. But when you're in the middle of it, you're thinking this is just so much bullshit, this is silly. That was around the time when we started discovering the anarchist critique. The main form at that point was Bakunin-style anarchism, based on the writing of revolutionary Russian philosopher Mikhail Bakunin, a general critique of hierarchy based on the outcome of the Bolshevik Revolution. But by then there were a lot of very authoritarian leftist organizations.

For the New Left, the central reference points in the period before the Vietnam War started in earnest had been about a kind of social criticism expressed in the early SDS (Students for a Democratic Society) statements and the original Port Huron Statement of June 15, 1962, which was basically democratic socialism, as well as being strongly antiwar and antiauthoritarian. Tom Hayden and Todd Gitlin where the primary players taking a critical look at daily life and social relations. People like Mark Rudd, the Free Speech activist and radical at Columbia, were an American version of Bolshevism. They hated the Communist Party for being Stalinist, but willingly or not they replayed the whole post-twenties and -thirties Russian Revolution again in America. The hippie counterculture was really laughing at these pompous buffoons because they thought they were silly. with their serious, authoritarian, unsexy behavior.

My best friend Steve Rees went off to Chicago in '68 and came back with an amazing portfolio of photographs and incredible stories of what happened. When you look back at it, I know historians called it the American version of Paris '68, but there wasn't a lot of radical content. It had all the limits of fair conventional protest and dissent. Trying to talk some sense to Power, trying to address the Democratic Party, or saying they were irrelevant, but still speaking to them. People got their heads bonked and they proved that a Mafioso like Mayor Daley is really a Mafioso. So, essentially, a lot of people who got very badly hurt to make a very small point.

In Santa Cruz a core started to form from the six to eight people of our little group to what later became the CEM (Council for the Eruption of the Marvelous). We agreed that the Left had become boring. Why were we so unhappy, we asked, doing what was supposed to be such an interesting activity? That was gnawing at us. We found out about the Up Against the Wall Motherfucker (UAW/MF) movement in New York and their anti-art critiques, and we were very excited by that. We'd been influenced by Jean-Luc Godard; we'd seen his films as they were coming out, with their interesting and comical critiques of bourgeois culture. Everyone thought 1968 was the big year, and I'm sure on the world stage it certainly was, but for me '69 was actually the year where everything happened. LSD came and went. It never disappeared, obviously, but it was replaced in large part by Meth as the drug of choice by 1969. The speed culture had taken over the Haight-Ashbury in San Francisco too. Even back then people were saying that was an intentional government conspiracy to hook people on a drug that was destructive rather than subversive, as some people found LSD to be.

Another benchmark moment of the movement was the birth of People's Park in Berkeley. That was in April of 1969. There was an unused area the university owned, behind Telegraph Avenue, that they had let go fallow. They were intending to build student apartments there. The mood on Telegraph Avenue had gotten darker. Right around that time Ronald Reagan, then governor of California, closed the state mental hospitals and emptied its thousands of beds, adding more chaos and drug use to the street population.

You've got this fallow land people are occupying, and sometimes living on it, and then the university decided, some say arbitrarily, to build dormitories right on that spot. The regents who ran the UC system were unhappy because they'd posted signs that said "Private Property," and these signs were being ignored. Reagan saw a chance to make his mark, and he decided to take the land back, whatever the cost.

One beautiful day with no warning, university workers put a cyclone fence around the park. The squatters tried to tear it down. They said this land now belonged to the people. The Left got very excited as they saw the Movement finally making a critique of private property and therefore capitalism. They were back to a real critique of the system in America, not the war in Vietnam. In effect they circled back. And it was powerful because people were exhausted with the distant abstraction of the war. How many times can you say those slogans? As horrible as the war was there was very little new content coming out in this critique at all. Here was a new twist. You had people highly mobilized by this idea that finally some territory has been freed, and the whole world could belong to us. We'll take it block by block.

Reagan wouldn't let this stand. The protest escalated and the governor upped the ante. There was a series of demonstrations, and in one of them a young man called James Rector was on top of a building, at the corner of Dwight Way, and the pigs shot a tear gas canister up and hit him in the head, and he died. This was a huge deal. Somebody had died in Berkeley. This was three years before Kent State. African-Americans were dying in riots in the ghetto, but white people weren't dying, it just wasn't happening. Nobody died in Chicago during the riots. James Rector had died, and all of a sudden things got huge. Masses of people were protesting everywhere. There was a big march organized against state violence. I remember going to a meeting at one of the leftist communes in Berkeley, and the self-proclaimed vanguards of the Left were unsure which way to go. They said, "We can't really appear to be manipulating this. Are we just going to have a peaceful demonstration or are we going to get violent?"

In the end the demonstration to take back the park was enormous and well organized, twenty thousand people marched peacefully in the streets around the campus. And even the university officials felt the state government's response went too far. Reagan called in the National Guard, and there were troops in People's Park with bayonets on their rifles, and tanks in the streets of Berkeley. This was a show of brute force. In a way it played into the hands of the Left. Reagan basically said, "If you attack private property, we'll kill you if we have to. Forget about the games you kids are playing, the student protests and all that. If you actually say this park belongs to you, that this city belongs to you, we're not going to let you do that."

The radicals in Santa Cruz, including me, were feeling a bit isolated from key events, even though we made the eighty-mile trip to Berkeley almost weekly. We decided that we should act to shed the peace-love label of UCSC, make a statement of solidarity, show that we weren't nonviolent after all. One of my friends and I agreed that we could pull the rug out from under the complacent students by attacking the campus police checkpoint at the entrance. It was isolated from the dorms yet sitting on the only road entering the school, visible to everyone who came through. Our plan was to make a Molotov cocktail and march through the woods from a mile off campus dressed in black and covered in dark face paint, set the checkpoint booth on fire, and then escape back down the hill to our car at two in the morning. Our chances of getting caught, we thought, were very low.

The day of the planned assault we met in a cottage behind the house

I shared with some other radicals. We decided to use a half-gallon jug for a larger effect than the typical wine bottle. We began pouring gas from a metal can through a funnel, and a few drops splashed on the concrete floor. Amateurs that we were we didn't notice that the pilot light on the small gas heater was on a few feet from us. After a couple of minutes the fumes exploded in a large fireball, and we ran out with our hair singed but happy to be alive. The wooden two-story structure became totally engulfed in flames, and we knew we were in deep shit. The firemen arrived and were unable to save the building. The police showed up to question us. Fortunately for us the heat was so intense it melted the glass bottle, so our story of gas spille as we were getting ready to fill a lawnmower was believed. Steve lost hundreds of photo negatives and most of his possessions. He forgave us generously when we told him our plan had failed. After that, when my co-conspirator and I walked on campus, there was a lot of snickering at our ineptitude among those in the know. Naturally, we hadn't really needed a Molotov cocktail, because we could have simply doused the structure with gas and lit it with a match. From that day on, I decided to leave the pyrotechnics to the pros. We were lucky we didn't suffer the fate of the Weather Underground bomb makers who killed themselves in a notorious townhouse fire in Greenwich Village in March of 1970.

 The year 1969 was a tumultuous, frantic, chaotic one in many ways. Santa Cruz really did live up to its reputation as a vortex of sex, drugs, and rock and roll. Academic life was, for many of us, a distraction from our focus on questioning every assumption of social relations. LSD, mescaline, and pot were almost free, and they were often the center of social events. Hard drugs were not around. There were plenty of mediocre bands playing on and off campus, and the Fillmore and Winterland music venues, which were in their glorious prime, were relatively close by to us, about a two-hour drive away. You could see the last of the great urban and country blues musicians, such as Muddy Waters, Lightnin' Hopkins, Jimmy Reed, Howling Wolf, John Lee Hooker, B. B. King, Bo Diddley, James Cotton, and Otis Redding. There was also the cutting edge jazz of Cannonball Adderley, Charles Lloyd, and Roland Kirk, along with nearly all of the legendary American groups, such as the Grateful Dead, Jefferson Airplane, Janis Joplin with Big Brother, Chuck Berry, the Byrds, Buffalo Springfield, the Doors, Sam & Dave, Sly and the Family Stone, Santana, CSNY, the Mothers of Invention, and Captain Beefheart. British rock bands and solo artists would also play locally, such as the Jimi Hendrix Experience, Eric Clapton, the Animals, the Yardbirds, Van Morrison, the Who, Procul Harum, Traffic, and Pink Floyd. These acts would perform in these two historic, open settings, with three wildly eclectic groups playing on a nightly bill for under $3. We were there almost every weekend and would crash on a friend's floor to avoid the drive home. It was a ritual. We almost didn't care who was playing. You had to be there.

But though these concerts were powerful emotional experiences, they mostly remained within the limits of cultural consumption: Stars performed, and the audience watched. Sex was another matter—it was participatory and not yet colonized by the mediation of sexologists or therapists or by the controlling influence of explicit sexual imagery in marketing and Internet pornography. We grew up without having ever having seen an explicit image of sexual activity. It was a territory to be explored, and the rules were being rewritten as we went along. Which was why it was so powerful when I met Elizabeth, who arrived in Santa Cruz in the winter of 1969 with the express purpose of developing a women's movement around UCSC. Elizabeth came from a commune in San Diego where Hebert Marcuse taught the theories of Wilhelm Reich, among other modern German radical intellectuals. Reich believed strongly in the liberating power of a healthy sex life. Among the books he wrote were The Function of the

Orgasm and The Mass Psychology of Fascism. Some of his books were banned in the U.S. for reasons having to do with his legal and moral battles with the courts, who tried to label him as mentally ill and dangerous when he was in fact bringing together science and pleasure, which struck at the heart of American Puritanism.

I met Elizabeth at a New Year's Day party at the home of a visiting Fluxus artist, Robert Watt. She was tall and elegant, and walked through the student crowd focused on her goal, which, that day, was to get laid. She approached me and wanted to know who the feminist leaders were on campus. I gave her a few names and she asked if I wanted to take a walk. We went outside into the garden that was wet from the rain. She led me to a secluded area and pushed me down. She quickly undressed me and herself and we made love. Even for Santa Cruz this was a quick buildup. She invited me back to her studio apartment, and I moved in for three months. Between sessions of hot sex we went out, focused on her mission of creating an active local women's liberation group. She talked to many women and a few men. She secured a meeting room on campus, printed literature, and created a reading list. As said, many people by then were tired of rehashing the antiwar talking points, and she attracted a fairly large group to the first meeting. They created an agenda, which included having the university add women's studies classes to the curriculum.

Elizabeth and I were inseparable initially. I was totally infatuated with her. She was so direct and serious, with a dark sense of humor. She appreciated my willingness to listen and to learn. She taught me the then evolving behavioral code for a man who respects women without patronizing them. She made the rules clear. We were together, which meant we weren't going to sleep with other people. It made sense. We were a dynamic bundle of energy with complementary knowledge, and we commanded a lot of respect in the radical community. But within a couple of months I broke our agreement and she immediately ended the relationship. I was devastated. She took up with another guy and I had to leave town for a few weeks. By the time I returned, she had gone back to San Diego.

I saw her again a year later. We had a romantic tryst on the beach in Santa Cruz, in plain sight of a bluff near a parking lot. I'm not sure if anyone saw us, but it added to thrill of the reunion. She told me that her group had decided to publish a pirate addition of Mass Psychology and needed money to print it. I had just inherited some money from my father's estate when I turned twenty-one. She had been sent by Lowell Bergman, a graduate student who was part of a group organizing sailors stationed at the headquarters of the Navy Pacific Fleet to desert the military. It was a highly risky tactic, with the threat of being charged with treason hanging in the air. I gave them the money because Elizabeth asked me. A few months after their photocopied edition of the Reich book was released, a commercial version appeared and they had to toss their books or risk being sued. A few years later I ran into Bergman, who was then an investigative reporter writing stories for Rolling Stone magazine. We met by chance in an elevator, and I asked him if he could repay the money which at the time he had called a loan. He snickered and said I gave the money to the Movement and he was not accepting personal responsibility.

In Santa Cruz, four of us who later became the Council for the Eruption of the Marvelous created a work group. We wrote a pamphlet that we printed in the thousands called The Nine Unnatural Acts of the University of California, referring to the number of campuses in the UC system. It was scatological, nasty, and very dark. It was also very poetic compared to everything else that was going on. In some ways it was a repetition of the Situationists, but in other ways the beginning of our Americanization of their ideas. We were excited to

be working together, discovering our power. At that point, we said we'd had enough. We were going off on our own. Our direction was going to be more toward the Situationists.

And then a surprising and tragic event happened that shaped the tone of our activity. One of the most liked and radical professors at Santa Cruz, an anthropologist named John Kroyer, committed suicide. That was a big deal. All the professors—among them Kenneth Tyman, who invented the core chemical that became Agent Orange—came to the local Unitarian church and gave lie-filled eulogies. They hated Kroyer because he had called their bluff, basically saying that not only were they not really peace-loving liberals, or radicals, but that they were complicit with the war effort through their research linked to the military-industrial complex.

We went back to our headquarters, where we'd written the Nine Unnatural Acts pamphlet, got really drunk, and just said, "Fuck it. This is too much. Let's screw with these guys." As a group, we decided that we were going to write something, which later became known as The Faculty Suicide Letter. The letter, in very flowery, aggressive prose, accused the teachers of being cowardly, monstrous, sexless liars. We suggested that they start killing themselves at the rate of one a month on a lunar cycle. We assigned different professors by names to different months. We put this letter in an envelope along with a razor blade for each of them, and signed it Tokyo Rose, the English speaking propagandist for Japanese overseas radio during World War II, and we dropped it in the campus mail.

We didn't hear that much about it until a few months later, when one of our comrades, William (Bill) Davis, who was involved in the whole affair and who hadn't graduated, was called in to the dean's office. Mark Hofstadter, the son of the pompous windbag Albert Hofstadter, who was named in the letter, had been going through Bill's book collection being a compulsive busybody. He had opened up an art book and the letter had fallen out. He read it and ran screaming from the room to tell his daddy what had happened. His father, paranoid prig that he was, called the FBI. He was going straight for the jugular. The dean told Bill, "You're facing expulsion for your role in this nasty business and the FBI has been called. They're down at the edge of campus and we don't know whether we should let them up or not, but they consider this to be a matter of domestic terrorism because you used the mail." Who knows if this was true? It seemed plausible at the time.

Back then, when most people were begging the faculty to help with their war protests, or to sign their petitions, it was pretty radical to make murderous threats against them using the mail. Eventually, one of the more liberal professors, a philosophy teacher called Maurice Nathanson, came to Bill's defense. His argument was this was part of a noble tradition of passionate, if ill-considered, intergenerational protest based on the traditions of Dada and surrealism. He even praised the style of the manifesto. Our friend, he said, had been overcome by a moment of passion and really didn't mean it, which was total bullshit. But the dean was convinced by the clarity of Nathanson's argument, and nothing happened to Bill, whom they were initially promising no disciplinary action only if he would roll over on us. If he had, we would've been arrested and our lives from then on would have been very different. As it turned out, the incident gave us a sense of invincibility that led us to Berkeley and many more devilish subversions.

Four

The year 1969 in many ways was a reconciling or settling of accounts from 1968, which everyone knows about in some detail because we're called the generation of '68. The dust was starting to settle, the counterculture was coming unhinged, the war continued at a great cost of lives. There was a show trial in 1968 that we basically ignored because it involved a bunch of Bolsheviks: the Black Panther Bobby Seale, the New Left author of the Port Huron Statement Tom Hayden, and several other activists—who were collectively known as the Chicago 8. They were put on a very public trial and eventually acquitted of conspiracy to foment the revolt during the Democratic National Convention. Obviously, they couldn't have started it or stopped it even if they'd wanted to; they were only the self-appointed spokespeople for the demonstrators, not their leaders.

Everyone was reading about the legal proceedings and watching the trial. Simultaneously in many cities there were continual court trials of the Black Panthers, and continual murders of and by Panthers. There was also an ongoing state-manipulated conspiracy, COINTELPRO (Counterintelligence Program), that targeted all left-leaning groups within the U.S. COINTELPRO was directed personally by J. Edgar Hoover at the FBI, under the direct orders of Richard Nixon, who had won the presidential election in 1968.

At the same time there was both the rise and fall in one year of the counterculture, between Woodstock and Altamont. It went from being a seemingly profound event, and a huge mass movement, to very dark and sinister period. The transition from psychedelic drugs to speed happened during that year, which influenced things greatly. But ultimately the hippies, like the opposition in general, failed because they had no ideas, no strategy, no vision. They only had slogans, such as "turn on, tune in, drop out." That was not a profound critique. It was a temporary lifestyle and certainly wasn't a sustaining concept.

The year 1969 was closing out, and I had been out of school for a year. In an existential moment I realized that it was the time to leave the college town where I had spent the last four years. I was at that age where you have to figure out what you're going to do with your life, and it sure as hell didn't mean a career, or even getting a job. It meant what act of revolt was next. That was our life trajectory. My partner Dan Hammer, with whom I later co–ghost wrote BAD: the Autobiography of James Carr, had gotten an internship at something called the New England Radical Printing Co-op. We all knew we had to have skills. I had already learned how to make 16mm black-and-white documentary films on a crude level with Steve. He and I had also hooked up with a national film collective called Newsreel that had access to films from Cuba, Vietnam, Algeria, and liberation movements in Africa. We showed these movies in fundraisers on campus, along with the classics of radical narrative film like The Battle of Algiers, Memories of Underdevelopment, and Godard's anti-colonial works from the sixties, like Le Petit Soldat.

Dan and I reasoned that if we were going to be propagandists in the proletarian tradition we had to be able to produce our own propaganda. It was a farm-to-table version of radicalism. We decided to go back East and see if we could do some printing at a real print shop. This was January of 1970, and as twenty-one year old dropouts we still had this delinquent bravado. We drove across the country from Los Angeles to Washington, DC, as fast as humanly possible. We had a Mercedes-Benz, a car that belonged to one of our friends' parents, and there were four drivers. We didn't stop to sleep. We barely stopped to go to the bathroom, and we drove across the U.S. in forty-two hours, including the stops. I've heard of someone doing it in thirty-eight, but it was still kind of world-class.

We ended up in Boston, and after a couple of days of listening to the vanguard party consciousness-building crap at the print shop—we were already anarchists and we really didn't like the bureaucracy of the New Left at all—we said, "Let's get out of here. This is boring." Yeah, things were happening really fast. We were not tolerating fools and routine. It was excruciating for us then. We didn't even tell them why we split. We were looking around for something to do when we heard that there was a building occupation at MIT. Even the nerds were in revolt, and they were imitating a very successful occupation at Columbia University a few months before where the students had broken into the office of the president. There was an iconic photo of Mark Rudd, one of the founders of the local SDS, in the president's chair smoking one of his cigars. They had pillaged the office and found a bunch of fairly incriminating documents in the files. This became the reigning model for taking over Daddy's house and "killing the father."

At MIT they announced they were going down the hall to the president's office, but since these guys were all geniuses, they forgot to take into account that he'd locked his door. They thought it was going to be open and they could just walk in. We were standing there laughing when two guys came up wearing full-face bank robber ski masks. They had a battering ram and we thought this was brilliant. This was like art, a happening. They battered the door down and the students ran in, and we thought the two most interesting people were those guys with the masks. When they ran out the door, we ran after them. We ran a few blocks and finally we said something like "Hey, are you the Situationists?" We thought, "Who else would be that clever?" And they said, "No, but we know them." And they stopped and took their masks off. We shook hands and introduced ourselves and they invited us to their house.

They had a group of five or six people, an odd collection, and they were called the Council for Conscious Existence (CCE). They had broken off from RAC (The Radical Action Collective at Columbia), and had been given all the Situationist translations from Tony Verlaan, who was a member of the American section of the SI (Situationist International). They invited us back to their apartment and we quickly learned they were crazy. It was kind of like a science fiction movie. They had a lot of money, there were some trust fund heirs there, but no understanding of the history of modern revolt, of the avant-garde, of anarchism. For them it was about spending money on expensive tools of communication and inventing self-affirming masturbatory rituals. They had a fancy color mimeograph duplicator, a technology that was soon replaced by the photocopy machine, to do color printing. They were producing something called The Daily Life Daily that consisted of the most minute detail about their lives. They idolized Raoul Vaneigem, the Situationist author of The Revolution of Daily Life. Essentially, they had gone to the deep cult level on Vaneigem. They were what we later called "Daily Lifeists." They printed a newspaper every day about the seven of them and what they did, what they had for breakfast, what they had for lunch, what they had for dinner. It was very elaborate in its details, and they would hand it around and read it. They also had these giant whiteboards everywhere with the calendar divided into four-day, sixteen-day, and sixty-four-day plans. They weren't really doing that much else, other than handing out leaflets and pamphlets that were excerpts from SI texts. Every time they left the house they were highly organized, like a military SWAT team, and they also had a specialized coded language. They called going to the grocery store a "probe into the spectacle," and they called a flashlight a "photon beam." It was all mostly the work of one fumbling narcissist called King Collins (that was his given name), and they followed him dutifully. He wasn't violent, or even that manipulative, he was just stupid.

What they did have were these translations of SI texts. Tony Verlaan had done some of them, and other amateur translators had done others. For us this was finding the holy grail. This was why we were there. They started handing out these translations one at a time. It was like getting the Bible or something. For a while we kind of went along with what they were saying. We stayed on good terms with them, and then immediately after that we went back to California. We now had the theoretical ammunition to start our own group. We came back to Berkeley at the end of January 1970. We had our group that a short time earlier had done The Nine Unnatural Acts. There was a crew, and Dan and I invited everyone to Berkeley to start a group.

My father's will stated that when I was twenty-one I was to receive my inheritance. I figured I was going to put my money where my mouth was. I rented a house in the Berkeley Flats and paid the initial expenses. The members were: Dan, a happy-go-lucky bon vivant from a prominent Democratic family in San Jose, a wisecracking guy but also a serious student of radical history who later became a speechwriter for Barbara Boxer, a well-known politician within the Democratic Party establishment; Bill Davis, an Andy Warhol–loving, heroin-using, nihilist Maoist, who had everything going on in a wildly eclectic patchwork, but also thought the Situationist ideas were interesting (He immediately proposed that we take the doors off the bathroom, which we did, for a while. He was that kind of guy. It was ridiculous. But that's the kind of thing that the Maoist criticism—that is, self-criticism—would have led to, because clearly, you're bourgeois if you have to wipe your ass in private.); Paul Mann, who had been a rock musician and was the best writer in the group, the editor, on his own, of an almost incomprehensible version of the 1966 Situationist classic On the Poverty of Student Life (I found out that there had been fifty-three translations in different languages by the time of its fiftieth anniversary year.); Stanley Ginsburg, who later became a high school teacher in South Central Los Angeles and was hardcore, without much of a theoretical background, but a complete risk taker, the bag man who would do anything, not that we did anything particularly dangerous. Then there were a couple of women who were our girlfriends and were not, I'm sad to say, treated as our equals. Wendy was the straight arrow wife of Paul Mann, and Kat lived with Bill and later became Terrence McKenna's partner and collaborator. That was the core group.

We had long discussions about what we would appropriate from the Council for Conscious Existence as part of our new agenda. Did any of their affectations really relate to how Situationists behaved? We guessed no. We created our own eclectic mix of almost equal parts surrealism, Dadaism, anarchism, and what we imagined to be Situationist theory brought to life. We immediately saw our strategic goal as a continuation of the critique of traditional leftism that the anarchists, composed of various groups and individuals, such as Up Against the Wall Motherfucker and Bakunin, had begun. We also saw our role as the introducers of Situationist ideas into the U.S. We were surrounded with a hodgepodge of groups: Maoists, Democratic Socialists, Trotskyists, the Black Panthers. We called them the false opposition. Unlike now, these people then had a real presence. They put out newspapers, books, and pamphlets, they ran bookstores. They were around everywhere on campus, at all the marches and demonstrations in the Bay Area. You could actually see them confusing people. Obviously, what was pushing them forward was the wave of hatred for the Vietnam War. It made perfect sense because in this country, especially in Black, Asian, and Mexican-American neighborhoods, there was a greater consciousness of Vietnam being ravaged by an occupying army.

In 1970 Cambodia was bombed, and there was a movement all over the United States, especially in California, against the expansion of the war. We set out to be playful because we loved Vaneigem, and we realized that we had to be funny, to enjoy ourselves. We wrote a series of leaflets that were a critique of various aspects of the Left. One featured the classic photograph of Che Guevara dead on the table. We were making a critique of martyrdom. It was an announcement for the "International Liberation School class on revolutionary embalming": "Why pay pig morticians when a plain pine coffin and a people's morticians will do?" We were trying to be funny and at the same time say that the ideology of sacrifice as practiced by the Left led to this. And we were alone in saying this of course, we were completely out there on a limb. This critique came from Totality for Kids by Raoul Vaneigem. Even today, if you make fun of a martyred Leftist figure, like a Cesar Chavez, people will lose their minds. I can only imagine people reading this kind of criticism and saying, "What is this shit? Why are you saying this? Don't you realize these people are on the same side as you are?" No, they were not. We did a critique of the Chicago 8 at the time they were on trial. We did a critique of the Black Panthers. We had Huey Newton looking like Jesus. We had a printing press in the basement, which we didn't know how to use very well. It was a large offset machine, and it was like, oh my God, there was ink and paper everywhere. Somebody, help us! And eventually a guy came along and said, "I like what you're doing. Let me move in and I'll become the printer." And he knew how to print. Our salvation had arrived.

We tried to be completely free in our lifestyle. We picked up a couple of things from the CCE. They did a lot of shoplifting. We stole our daily necessities in a very systematic way. We had decoys who went into the Safeway supermarket looking like they were stealing but then not steal. Then we had a couple dressed up in very conservative clothes, Paul Mann and his wife Wendy, and they would grab the steaks and the French wine and walk calmly out of the store. We were about the practice of theory, the theory of practice. We were about implementing radical ideas in daily life, living them, but also having a real critique of the spectacle, the Situationist critique.

We found another printer with his own clandestine basement shop who was a real free spirit, and he was producing various forms of fake identification, which back then were simply funny, not serious at all. The California driver's license then had a black-and-white photo, and on the back of the license there was a little green seal. He provided everyone with a lot of these. We had a lot of fun making up our aliases, because we could be anybody, martyrs from proletarian history, rock stars. And that opened certain doors to rent certain things. We didn't return them. We outfitted a lot of our lifestyle that way.

Much to our surprise, we did some other things that I think actually influenced the world of art. We made some trading cards, and before that the only trading cards you could buy were baseball or football cards. No one had played with this form at all, which now has been used a lot. We decided we were going to do these trading cards that made fun of social roles and social institutions. They were called in In the Void trading cards, and there were team cards like "the faculty" and "the nuclear family." Those were the teams. And then there were individuals like Johnny B. Goode, who was a peace corps volunteer, and Petulia Bourgeois, who sold beads on Telegraph Avenue. We were poking fun at all this, and we had pictures on the front of the cards and description on the back, the same size as a baseball card. We printed about three or four hundred of these and went out one day on Shattuck Avenue in Berkeley and handed them out. And people just went crazy. They were chasing us for them—the construction workers, everyone—they were all reading these cards and we could've sold thousands, but it was in the moment.

We also wanted to reach out to the real proletariat, not just the students and intellectuals. We wrote a leaflet addressed to people living in a suburb of San Jose called Parktown. We wrote this very dark in some ways, cynical, plea to them to abandon their homes and move out. There was a tranquilizer back then called Milltown, so we said, "leave Milltown leave Parktown, leave your husbands, your children, leave your life behind, flee." We had the same team, Paul and Wendy, that looked so wonderfully like Jehovah's Witnesses. They went out there dressed in conservative, Republican Party outfits. We were manipulating and playing with social roles, based on Vaneigem's critique, the "Yes Men" thing. We were consciously trying to see if we could experiment with pulling out the rug from under people's ideas of how a normal person should behave or look. They went around and handed out hundreds of these sheets. The title of the leaflet was Is This Our Fate? We didn't put a return address on there, which was smart or dumb—I don't know which. Not surprisingly we never got any feedback, it was just the idea. The other thing is when we were writing stuff like this, we would spend an entire hour or two every day just laughing. We did quite a lot of that. This activity was funny, and it was fun. We were having a really good time. We weren't working. We were all doing this full-time thanks to my inheritance, subsidized by the shoplifting. It was an orgy of radical playful behavior. It was addictive. There were a lot of other collective living groups at the time. There was a Leftist house called COPS (Citizens Against Police Surveillance). It was up by the university campus. But they were all traditional

Bolsheviks.

We started to get a lot of attention because we were out there doing this stuff nobody else was doing at that moment. People came to us. And one of the people who showed up quite early on was Ken Knabb, who later became well known for translating the works of the SI. A lot of people wanted to meet us, but we were pretty careful because we met some really crazy people, psychotic, but not dangerous. Ken found us about four months after we started, and he said, "You guys are really cool." We said, "Yeah, we're cool." We had him over, and he said, "How does this work?" At that time he was a Buddhist anarchist—he still is. One of us said, "You're really incoherent." That was our word meaning you're not a Situationist, meaning you're full of shit. We told him, "We don't really want to hang out with you unless you write a public critique of what you're doing now and hand it out." This was Maoist style self-criticism, a mild version of that. It was more like a high school club basically. We said to Ken, "All right, you know, write this because otherwise you're just so incoherent. We really can't hang with you." A week later he showed up and there was his critique. But we were never really that close with Ken because he had a very dry personality and he wasn't that playful. We saw he was very serious. He was bright and capable and obviously a good writer and all that, but he wasn't someone we wanted to hang with because we were all different from that. We were the cool crowd.

We heard from the kids at Point Blank magazine, which later evolved into Processed World: Chris Winks, Chris Shutes, and David Jacobs,. They were three or four years younger than us. They were in high school in Palo Alto and had written critiques of high school life and were looking to do more. Other than these meetings with various groups, we were kind of alone for that period. We were open to doing anything. We pretty much tried to be a mouthpiece for the Situationists. We tried to think, "What would the Situationists do if they were here?" Jean-Luc Godard, who in retrospect I think was an extremely interesting filmmaker, also said many stupid things in his films, but he was a good artist and he influenced me and my work. He came to the Berkeley Community Theater to show a film that was called British Sounds (also called See You at Mao), one of his more radical Marxist films, although he made many movies during this period. We thought, "What would the SI do? Throw tomatoes at him." We organized an intervention. One of his films was called Le Mépris (Contempt). We wrote a leaflet about it in English, then we translated it into French, and the French side said the opposite of what the English side said. Don't ask me why we did that, but each side was completely the opposite of the other. And then we had Dan dress up as a priest because Luis Buñuel hated priests and Dan looked a bit like a Jesuit. It was funny to have him dress up in a priest's cassock, which we rented, and throw tomatoes at Godard. We showered the audience with this leaflet, but we missed with the tomatoes, sadly. There was an article in the Berkeley Barb a few days later that said, "Why didn't they stop and talk to us? We could have had a debate," which in a way might've been really interesting. Maybe we blew it.

There was a plan and there were plans, but then there was what was fun to do. We did have our own whiteboard where we had strategies that were all mapped out, and we would sit around and discuss them, but there was also just the impulse of the moment. One of the ways we decided we could subvert commodity fetishism was by printing counterfeit concert tickets. I think we did three sets. We did the Berkeley Jazz Festival with the same printer who had done the driver's licenses. He was a master printer for the time. He wasn't an engraver, he didn't counterfeit money, but he was high-level. We printed a set of tickets for the Rolling Stones at Winterland and they were five colors. It took a long time to print these and we would hand out these tickets. People were in shock. They kept saying, "Can't we give you money?" We said, "No, we don't want money." We told them we were there to realize the spirit of the gift. We also drove through East Oakland handing out five hundred tickets to the Berkeley Jazz Festival. These were all non-reserved seating, so we could get away with it. But we did do a Chuck Berry revival at the Berkeley Community Theater where the seats were reserved. We had to run around getting chased by ushers because we kept finding empty seats and then people kept showing up with our tickets. Eventually, after a few Keystone Cop moments, we had to leave.

Paul Mann wrote in his own Dadaist, surrealist way. One of his works was a pamphlet called On Wielding the Subversive Scalpel, about détournement, the Situationist idea of taking existing cultural and political elements and using them against themselves. This pamphlet showed a lack of understanding of the difference between art and criticism, but despite that flaw it was an interesting text and had some great illustrations. As an example of our use of subversion we changed billboards, which a decade later became a stylized, ritualized anti-art art form through the Billboard Liberation Front, who offered mediocre, harmless satire of fast food and cigarettes as content. They dealt with the obvious excesses and left the operating principles of the commodity untouched. Whereas Dan found an airline billboard that said "Los Angeles, $29, five flights a day," and he simply added the word "Why?" We knew we were pioneers, and we took that responsibility very seriously during that period.

One highlight from 1970 was the response to the war in Cambodia and the protests that included Kent State University that same year. Four people were killed at Kent State in May when the National Guard opened fire on the students who were protesting the Kissinger- and Nixon-engineered carpet bombing of Cambodia and Laos. There was a series of protests at

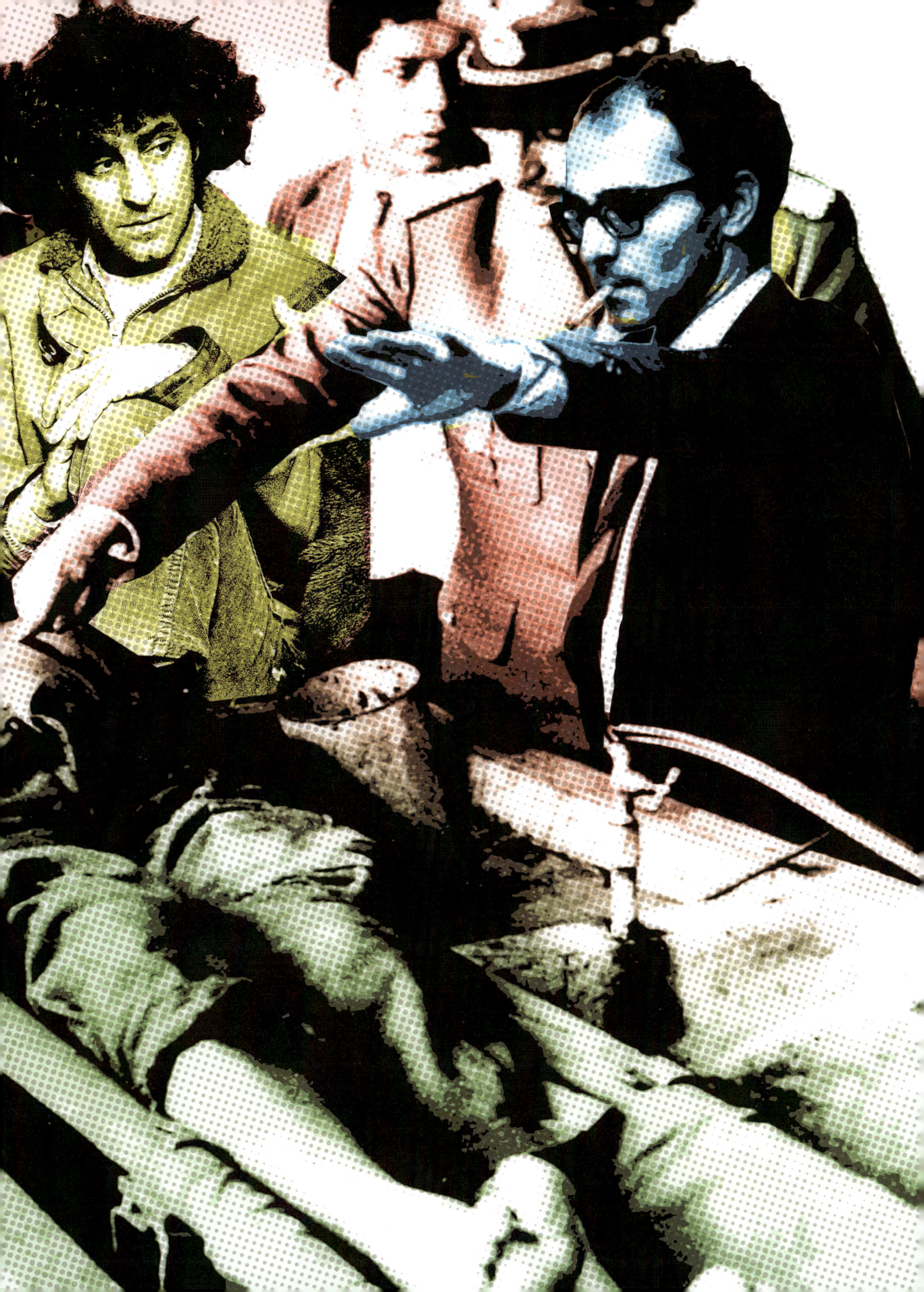

all the University of California campuses at the same time. We organized a probe, borrowing from the CCE, around the state of California, to recruit new members. We skipped Santa Cruz. We'd had enough of that place. We'd already demolished it. We thought there was nothing left standing. We showed up in Santa Barbara, this very bucolic California beach town. Strangely enough, they had a very one-off event where drunk surfers and nihilist beachcombers burned down the local Bank of America. We came there just right after this happened. Nearby Isla Vista was a hub of fun and adolescent activity, mainly drinking and surfing. We were thinking, "Okay, who are the instigators? Can we find some people to talk to?" All we had to go on was this one very radical, extreme act of burning down the bank. The unexpected highlight of the statewide trip was UC San Diego, where we found recruits for our cause. That year a student named George Winnie, who had previously shown no interest in protests, had burned himself to death, like a Buddhist monk, right on the campus.

At that point, arguably the most radical professor in the country, and the New Left's senior intellectual, was Herbert Marcuse. He was teaching at UCSD and had written a book called One-Dimensional Man that attempted a fusion of Freud and Marx, the soup that everyone was trying to swim in, bringing the personal and the political together. His book was a bestseller, and it was the most serious philosophical book produced in America that tried to talk about mass culture as alienation. He was also one of the least interesting members of the Frankfurt School. There were some brilliant thinkers in that group, among them Adorno, Horkheimer, and Gunter Anders. But Marcuse was courageous in many ways as he stood up for a lot of radicals. It was certainly better to have him there than not.

Marcuse had some graduate students he'd cultivated. One was Lowell Bergman, who had taken my money for the Reich book and who later became

a producer on the successful television show 60 Minutes, the journalist who was immortalized by the Al Pacino performance in the film The Insider. He was a radical back then, and would also go on to be one of the major forces at the UC Berkeley School of Journalism. And then there was a guy called Bill Netzer, who was extremely bright and later helped Dan and me rewrite Bad. Netzer became part of our coterie based on this trip. But the probe wasn't terribly successful. That was the beginning of the end for the group, in fact. We realized that this movement wasn't growing out the door, and that Berkeley was a more receptive climate in many ways.

We were invited to a party at the home of Mark Messer, a mealymouthed liberal professor of sociology. When we attended these events, we were in full attack mode, sparing neither teachers nor students. Several years back Messer had flunked me when Ron Berger handed in my term paper late. I had gone off to Europe with my girlfriend and asked him to deliver it in my absence. It caused me a great deal of inconvenience, and I never forgave Messer. Why stand on ceremony when the world is falling apart? We were hanging around his Victorian house drinking a better grade of red wine and nibbling on brie and rye crisps when his wife Kathy came up to me. She looked like a graduate student, with a worldly air, no makeup, long hair pulled back, wearing jeans and a loose pullover sweater. She asked me what we were doing in Berkeley, and I told her we were working on destroying the spectacle. That intrigued her and we arranged to meet for coffee. The coffee part lasted a few minutes and we rushed back to the CEM house, where we spent many days thereafter in bed. Finally, one night, at 2 a.m., as part of pillow talk I confessed my role in the suicide letter and told her that her husband had failed me.

A dead silence was followed by her getting quickly out of bed. Kathy said, "So this is a revenge fuck. You used me to get even, you immature little shit. You're nothing but a seducer with a nasty agenda. So much for all your pretentious rhetoric. You hate women like all the rest of them." She ran from the room and that was the last I heard from her.

Paul was up in the living room reading. He looked up as she stormed past. "That ended well," he said.

"Clearly I fucked up," I answered.

"Truly. She now knows what we did and could turn us in," Paul responded, and then he continued turning on me. "I've been meaning to talk to you. It's like you are out of control. Not all the time, obviously. But you let your demons take over. There's some dark shit in you with your dad. Shit you haven't addressed."

I answered with a snicker, "Oh, right. This coming from the author of the Go Kill Yourself letter."

Paul had a readymade response: "But you notice I channel my anger into socially disruptive and therefore useful forms."

We both laughed. He had touched a nerve. I thought out loud, "Things happen so fast around here. It's so intense. I can't live this way twenty-four hours a day. I feel like I'm going crazy."

By June the fissure lines between all of us had become apparent. There were more disagreements about the difference between artistic activity and Situationist criticism. The artistic spirit reemerged especially in the being of Paul Mann. And Bill Davis brought up his affinity for Maoism. We started to fight more and get less done. Action had been the glue that held us together. Paul and his girlfriend moved out. Soon after they broke up. Dan stuck around for a while then went back to San Jose for the summer. Bill drifted away.

And then a funny thing happened. Some of us who had recently graduated got mailed cards by the credit card companies without us requesting

them. Visa, Mastercard didn't exist back then. These were gas company credit cards. We figured we didn't ask for them, but we could use them. Could they make us pay? Imagine how much the world has changed—how naive companies were back then giving away credit cards to millions of people, most of whom just cut them up. We used mine to take a free trip across America. I had a Volkswagen bus, so Stanley Ginsburg and I decided we were going to take our existential voyage of discovery across America. We were going to do our Easy Rider pilgrimage as a swan song to the CEM.

We left the house. I paid the last month's rent on our six-month lease. We drove through the South via Route 66, freewheeling. We got to New Orleans and rented an apartment in a beautiful old building. We thought we were going to stay there a month. It was mid-summer and really hot. Stanley was extremely eccentric. He decided he was only going to eat three foods for every meal on the entire trip. He did some research and decided it was going to be jack cheese, watermelon, and raisins. He ate that three times a day doing cleanses. He was an early practitioner of health foods and cleanses.

And I thought "Okay, I'm not doing that, but if you want to, be my guest." I wasn't a foodie then, but I was in New Orleans, so we started hanging out and drinking. We had this nice apartment. I must've had my money still. We met a cool jazz musician, and I remember his first name was James. He was a saxophone player and he'd just gotten out of prison. We went over to his apartment. This was really out of a film. On the table was a newspaper and the photo on the front page of the Picayune was headlined "Two Women Escape from City Jail Wanted for Murder." Those two women were sitting on the bed. We said, very calmly, "It's time to go," and politely excused ourselves. But in order to have a little fun, we literally found the Hell's Angels, and there were two weeks left on our lease, so we gave them the keys to the apartment. We had a great time and returned to the Bay Area.

In September of 1970 Dan and I decided to go to Europe on a few days' notice. Back then there were planes that were chartered by travel agents. They would book a plane and charge $150, $200 for a round-trip to Europe. Our goal was to meet the Situationists. We said enough is enough. We had met the fake Situationists. Where were the real ones? We were going to show up with all of our cool shit. We brought all the stuff that we'd done. We thought this would impress them. We deserved a meeting with the Situationists.

We had one introduction, from a woman who later became my girlfriend and had come over and been friends with the printer, the crazy printer. She knew one of the beau barracadier, the dashing street fighters who really threw the Molotov cocktails in 1968. He was part of the extended SI circle and his name was Alan. We figured we were going to get to meet the Situationists through him. We landed in England and stayed with Stuart and David Christie. I remember one of the highlights of that trip was that they had a coin-operated power box in their apartment. You had to keep feeding the meter, and it went out several times when we were there. They showed us London.

Eventually we made it to Paris, after a two-week detour in Amsterdam. We met Alan and he said "I will present your credentials." It was like a diplomatic meeting at an embassy. Everyone wanted to meet the SI people. If you can imagine, they were considered to be the most important modern, libertarian radicals in the world. They were partially responsible for, and took credit for, almost bringing down the government of France. And they were cool dudes with this radical critique, so who wouldn't want to meet them? We handed Alan all of the stuff that we'd brought over. He came back and he said: "Yeah, you know, okay—they said okay."

We went to a restaurant in the Latin Quarter and we were saying, as we walked in, "Where's fucking Guy Debord?" He was one of the founding members, but he didn't come, and of course Vaneigem had a better excuse because he lived in Belgium. The other three French Situationists came though, and Alan said this was a positive response. This was like diplomacy; you read the signs and meaning in the cinema. There was Rene Viénét, Rene Riesel, and Christian Sebastiani. They were there playing the part, dressed in ascots, leather coats—very dashing, very chic. All the conversation was in French so we were okay, but not great. They were really interested in us. They wanted to know what was going on in America because they had not gotten any news from the American section in a very long time. By then the American section consisted of Jonathan Horelick and Tony Verlaan—that was the core group that was left. There were two others that had been excluded, Robert Chasse and Bruce Elwell.

But what was so cool was they said, "We want to send you on a diplomatic mission." We were thinking at that point that we were basically taking over from the American section. They asked us to go to Spain because they had been receiving some interesting inquiries. We said, "Why don't you just phone them?" They said, "We've tried to call them, but no one ever answers." We jumped on the train and went to Barcelona on a diplomatic mission for the SI! We were thinking we had all read about the First International, we knew what was going on. We felt like we were part of the Russian Revolution. We were under the sway of these guys. This was sexy and fun, this was completely cool. They had taken us in. The pages from history we had read had come to life and we were living them.

When we got to Barcelona, we couldn't find the Spanish guys. We had gone seven hundred miles on the train, and we knocked on the apartment door and nobody answered. We keep knocking and nothing. We stayed overnight and came back the next morning, same thing. We hopped on a train back to

Paris. We were willing to do anything. We were also in Europe, of course, and so we were having fun, goofing around, and meeting people on the train.

We returned to Paris and were hanging out with Alan. The sad thing was that Alan was living with this incredibly rich woman in this extraordinary apartment on Île de le Cité, one the most glamorous and expensive parts of the city, on an island in the middle of the Seine. She was really beautiful and fun, but he was incredibly depressed because the revolution hadn't happened. Maybe he had other reasons to be a depressed drunk, but he was a drunk. Along with a lot of other people he had been convinced that the revolution was coming. The tidal wave swept onto the beach and then it went out and it never came back.

We met the Situationists a few more times in various bars and restaurants in Paris. Viénet was to me the most interesting. He was a scholar on Chinese History. He had incredible knowledge and references, and also had books in English—one of them I remember was Oriental Despotism by Karl Wittfogel. Vienét gave me a reading list about that part of the world. He was not a beau barracadier. Riesel and Sebastiani were the militants within the Situationist camp.

What I soon realized was that they needed a marketing department. They had, as Ken Knabb would later say, written everything they needed to write. They had done the theoretical part. Now it was time to spread the word. They recruited a bunch of people, like Tony Verlaan, who were charismatic and not going to write much, but who appeared to live the revolution. They were like movie stars, cocky, self-absorbed. They were literally getting dozens of people coming from all over the world to meet them, but people like Guy Debord never went out to these meetings.

They gave us more translations, more books, and we told them we were thinking of going back. We had been there for several months and it had been fun, but now we needed to tell everybody in America what was going on. We thought at that point because they were complaining about not having any output or contact from the official American SI, and on the other hand they liked us a lot, that it seemed obvious we were going to be added to the American section, or even replace it altogether. We had obviously executed their orders, their diplomatic mission to Spain. We had proven to be willing foot soldiers. We were the right guys for the right job at that moment. They said, "You've got to go to New York and check on Horelick and Verlaan. We want a full report on their status. We need you to do that." And they trusted us. You have to remember, we thought that there was going to be a revolution, and while all this stuff that we were doing was not going to make a huge difference, it was part of it, it was part of the necessary steps to expand the international revolution. At our age most people hadn't done much, they were still in college. We were out plotting to destroy the spectacle.

We went to New York. We found Horelick's place in Brooklyn. We knocked on the door and Horelick answered. There was a woman there and it was incredibly tense. It was like we'd walked in on something. What was going on? Horelick said, "You can't believe what's happened. Don't ever fall in love with a mafia don's daughter."

I said, "What are you talking about?"

He said, "I've got a contract on my life! My girlfriend is the daughter of a major mafia don in New York, and he wants to kill me because he knows I'm some kind of bad news—we're leaving tomorrow for upstate New York. I don't know when I'm going to be back, but I can't stay here."

I was thinking, "So that's why you haven't written anything in months." I told him the Situationists in Paris were wondering what was up.

And he said, "I've just been too nervous."

We met Tony Verlaan separately in New York, and I realized that he was one of these classic Dutch guys. Because their language is even weirder than German, they have to learn foreign languages and, somehow or other, they have an incredible ability to master them. Tony, without exaggeration, was fluent in French, English, German, Spanish, and Italian, but he couldn't write a single sentence in any of them. The combination of the two guys was devastatingly unproductive. The SI had a really weak American section there, and all we had to do was to send back the news. We wrote to the SI in France and we got an answer of "Well, you know, we'll think about it."

As it turned out at that moment the SI was in a state of devolution, and by the next year Debord had written Veritable Split in the International and the group self-destructed. The organization fell apart for a lot of good and bad reasons. Looking back with a more objective eye on those two years, I'd say our most important contribution to the radical dialogue of the time was our critique of the New Left based on fundamental Situationist principles. This led to a passionate denunciation of the rigid, hierarchical, Christian militancy of sacrifice. We attempted to truly Americanize the Situationist critique in our own way. We never stopped trying to be humorous, playful, lighthearted. We took ourselves seriously on one level, but on another level we were consistently self-deprecating. We showed a willingness to address ordinary people, even though I'm sure in many instances they didn't understand what we were doing. We thought that people were really suffering from the boredom of suburban life, and if we just said the magical words they would join us, in the same way we had found the magical words that changed our lives as Situationists. It was a kind of religious thing. We didn't sleep. We stayed up all night. Every day was a new challenge. Every day was a new leaflet. Every day was a new subversive move. We were running day and night as if the world was about to end. That was the frenzy we were in. So much happened that I can't believe we did all of it in one year.

In some ways we didn't really radically extend the SI critique, but in other ways I think we set a kind of standard for how to take European material and bring it into an American context. I'm not sure that many people who followed after us did a very good job with that. In terms of pure inventiveness we were more adept, I think, partly because we were still close to 1968 and the kind of naivete and enthusiasm that had permeated that time, and that feeling of optimism hadn't really faded. It was infectious right at that moment. But the further you got from that, the more things got difficult, and the more things devolved.

Five

1971 through 1972 was a transitional period for a lot of reasons. It was clear that the wave that had hit the world in 1968 had crashed, and it was beginning to be obvious that the euphoric moment that we'd extended for two years was over. We had to figure out a new direction, but we weren't quite ready to do that. In the rock-and-roll world a lot of bands calling themselves supergroups were forming in order to commercialize the spirit of Woodstock. What if we could put together a meeting of the minds of the most groovy Situationists in the Bay Area and form a new group, a supergroup, to take on a critique of the Left and the counterculture? Obviously we could, because what was keeping us from doing it? No one was talking about working, we weren't going to school. We were freelance. I was still living off my tiny inheritance, and other people were getting by on almost nothing. Our expenses were so low that even if the others didn't have an inheritance, they were spending a couple hundred dollars a month to live, so anyone could join the band. Setting the stage were Dan Hammer and I, from the Council for Conscious Existence. We had gone off to Europe together and come back after having met the Situationists and realizing we weren't going to become the American section of the SI because, unbeknownst to us at that moment, the SI was coming apart.

We hadn't heard much from France, so we thought we should focus on America. We formed our supergroup: There was Ken Knabb, our Don Quixote, who had made his appropriate self-criticism the year before, and his Sancho Panza was Ron Rothbart. Both had attended Shimer College in Illinois. Knabb became the official docent and defender of the Debord legacy which had no real challengers, and Rothbart became a green tourist nature photographer. And there were two other guys, a Bookchinist (a follower of the American anarchist Murray Bookchin) named Michael Lucas, who was a big gay rights advocate and who later died of AIDS. He was one of the few dancing, nightclubbing disco Situationists. He wasn't much of a writer, but he was fun and enthusiastic. And then there was a guy called John Adams, no relationship to the ex-president of the United States. He had a big beard and he was straight, and kind of academic. Our goal as stated was to create the most complete critique of the New Left movement, which included SDS, Up Against the Wall Motherfucker, the Weather Underground, and the hippie counterculture. And we wanted to include a critique of the pseudo critique of society by Alvin Toffler in his bestseller Future Shock. This was an incredibly ambitious project, at least the way we set out to do it, which was going to be as brilliant as On the Poverty of Student Life and as comprehensive as Herbert Marcuse—altogether a huge task.

Dan and I were the activist side. We wanted to get something out there. We thought it was really important, whereas Knabb and Rothbart were much more self-critical and would constantly find things wrong with the writing. We had endless meetings where people presented drafts and found reasons to rewrite them. And it was all authored uncredited, it was collaboration. At the same time, fortunately for us, there was an active labor movement in San Francisco. There were three principle strikes in 1971: There was the cable car workers wildcat strike where the workers went against their transportation union and went out on strike, and a lot of them were African-American, very militant. Cool. They had these incredible hipster looks and they were doing the cable car thing. They had this routine playing the bells. They went on strike for higher wages. There was a social worker's union wildcat strike almost at the same time, and it turned out that one of the leaders of that strike was John Zerzan. Zerzan founded a leaflet, actually it was a comic, that we did called Wildcat Comics. We met with some of these people and we handed the leaflet out. It was pretty funny and was actually an improvement on the SI detournement of comics in some ways. It had some comical images in it from I Am A Fugitive From The Chain Gang, a classic film from the 1932. The cable car drivers were not happy with what we did. They thought we were homing in on their world and providing too much of a radical critique for what were bread-and-butter issues for them.

We did meet John Zerzan and we went through the same routine as with Knabb. He found us, we found him, I can't remember which, and he was defending his reformist position and we said, "Yeah, okay you know if you want to have any more conversations with us you'll have to make a critique of that." And he made the critique. I'm not sure if it was written to us, but we started hanging around after that. Then there was a big strike of the telephone workers. They were on strike for nine months, the CWA, the Communications Workers of America, and they won most of their demands. We included them in our critique in a couple of these leaflets, in conjunction with the guys from Point Blank because by now we were fast friends. Between us and Point Blank, we were the Situationist movement in the Bay Area, so we thought we were this presence, the radical rulers of the Bay Area. Anything that happened, we had to comment on it; any event we were a part of, any situation, we had to provide the Situationist perspective on what was going on. And we did, pretty much, as we were very active in that period.

Starting in 1971, and into 1972, there was a wildcat strike at an automobile assembly plant in Ohio called Lordstown that was very radical. There was a lot of violence. They went against the UAW (United Auto Workers), which was very unusual, as it was an incredibly powerful union then, but they went out on strike and they didn't win. It was a very militant period. And there was also a postal strike that happened the next year. There was a wildcat strike that started in New York because the postal workers didn't have the right to collective bargaining. At that point, Nixon ordered the army and the National Guard to deliver the mail. People forgot this direct intervention. It took ten times as many soldiers to deliver the mail as it had postal workers. It was total chaos. The stock market dropped dramatically, and there was even talk about closing Wall Street temporarily to prevent a disaster. We were thinking maybe this was '68 again. We were a dreamy group, and this seemed like the power of the unions to affect the stock market could be disseminated further. The strike spread nationally, but sporadically. For eight days the postal service was disrupted, and back then we didn't have FedEx, or things like it. The U.S. Mail was the only game in town, so it was a big deal. This was a much more interesting movement to look at than the anti-Vietnam protests because it was following the blueprint the Situationists had laid out for a worker-student alliance, or worker-intellectual alliance. We were competing with every other Trotskyist and Bolshevik group, and the embarrassing thing was they were saying very similar things. They were defending the wildcat strike. We didn't seem that cool in a way. And that gave us pause.

The other way that the movement extended itself beyond traditional worker protest was in the penal system. There was a non-student, essentially non-white movement rising up in the prisons. In 1971 they were clearly influenced by the Black Panthers because the third world critique—of colonization and slave labor—if it made sense anywhere made sense in the inner cities. A lot of the Panthers had come out of prison stays, and there was a free flow of information between inside and outside on the streets. The convict who individually made the biggest impact at that point, and is still remembered in some circles, was George Jackson. Jackson had been in prison for a long time. He'd committed armed robberies. No one was questioning that. He wasn't one of those guys who claimed he was innocent. In a way he was proud of the fact that he'd done it. He had read Jean Genet and had been influenced by his very passionate critique of the French prison system. His plea for prison reform touched the heart of many white liberals. He was their guy because he was very literate and had a literature background. He was kind of a hodgepodge of, aside from Genet, Frantz Fanon, Maoism, Malcolm X, and the Black Panthers. That was the stew that he put together. It wasn't really coherent, but it was very angry, and there was poetry in it. It definitely mobilized a lot of people, but we didn't really know how to respond to Jackson's plea for justice. It was clearly reformist because it was focused on improving prisons without calling for their abolition. It was also part of the Black Panther movement, and we were definitely the enemies of the Black Panthers.

In our idea of all that was wrong with the radical movement we were looking to blame the failure of it on the inadequacies of the Left. Even though we called them the pseudo-left from the very beginning, we were at the same time saying, well, they could have done better. They should have done better. It was a really fundamental obfuscation of the problem that we were confronting, which was that our theory, our ideas, our critique, and our lives, were inadequate to the task, and to project this on to others was bad faith. In a way, that's why we never published this theory, because we realized that what we really were doing was blaming this movement for our failure. We weren't capable of addressing these inadequacies. Fortunately, ideas came along from Europe once again that helped us with that. But we didn't have the humility or the ability to really take this on with our limited resources.

If this worker unrest hadn't come along, we would have even dissolved sooner because we were at complete loggerheads. Fortunately, we found our way out of that. And the way out was that Dan Hammer's sister, Betsy, was someone who had a romantic and political attraction to black militants. Before she met and married James Carr, she had another black militant boyfriend who had been very active in the Venceremos Brigade. Their house in San Jose was a very cozy middle-class home, and it became the center for ex-Venceremos veterans. The Venceremos Brigade were the anti-imperialists who volunteered to go to Cuba and cut sugarcane. They were a mixed group of white and black leftists. And it was backbreaking work in the tropical heat. It was the hardest work ever. They would come back exhausted, but exalting Cuba, and they all had great stories, none of which appealed to us because we knew Castro was a Stalinist who killed the anarchist opposition. We used to have huge verbal fights in the house. We could literally almost not go in there. There was the Situationist contingent in one part of the kitchen and then all the African-Americans and Betsy in the other part of the kitchen, each group hurling insults at the other.

Betsy met Jimmy Carr through her prison activism. He had been in jail with George Jackson and had spent most of his adult life there. He had been a bank robber and she loved this guy. He had been paroled to UC Santa Cruz with the help of an African-American professor, Herman Blake. Jimmy was a total autodidact and had taught himself how to do calculus in prison. He got a teaching assistant position at Santa Cruz, yet he had never even gone to high school, let alone college. He was in the California penal system from the time he was twelve. This was the period when African-American militants were very sexy. We were all into free love, but we went in the front door. Jimmy had a key chain that he pulled out, and on his key chain there were thirty keys—they all belonged to different women who had given him their house keys so he could come in anytime he wanted. As Jimmy explained, it was based on Fidel Castro, because in Cuba, women, according to Jimmy and the other black militants, always left the back door unlocked in the hope that Fidel would show up. Apparently, he occasionally did show up. Talk about crazy sexuality. Jimmy was a very handsome guy. He'd been a world class weightlifter, literally bench pressed six hundred pounds. His chest was so developed, you could put a glass of water on each of his pecs and it would sit there.

Betsy fell in love with this guy, and we were hanging out there because it was part of our route and we went there for a home-cooked meal. Dan's mother had a strong affinity for George Jackson. She was a passionate correspondent with him. Some of her letters, I think, are in the Soledad Brother book. We met Jimmy and didn't quite know what to make of him at first, although the immediate appeal was, okay, here's a real radical. One of the first conversations we had was about Malcolm X. I was on my high horse, so I said Malcolm was cool but he wasn't really that radical. And there was silence and there's this guy sitting there, and he couldn't even wear regular pants because his legs were so massive he had to wear overalls, and he had a shaved head covered by a cap, and he looked at me and said, "You know, I could just break your neck." and Dan jumps up and he says, "Oh no. Isaac is sometimes very irrational." But it turned out that even though it was a stupid thing to say, and it wasn't even true, because I was this white guy saying that, trying to be honest, it actually broke the ice. It made him think this guy is wrong, but at least he speaks his mind. We started hanging out, which back then meant smoking dope and drinking rum and smoking cigars—all from Cuba.

I was twenty-three and Dan was a year younger, Jimmy was thirty. He started telling the most incredible stories. They were in Soledad Prison in the Salinas Valley in 1958, and they started a riot just for fun. They ran into the shower in the gym, and so the officials, not wanting to mess with them, called the local National Guard. They started shooting into the shower and they shot every tile off the wall. But then they realized that Jimmy was only 17, and if they killed him as a juvenile, he wasn't even supposed to be in Soledad, he was there illegally, so there would be hell to pay. The guards said, "Come on out, we're not going to kill you guys." They were going to kill them, the cons thought. But with Jimmy there, they simply locked them in solitary for a few weeks and everyone lived to fight another day.

He told stories that we were sure no one had ever heard. We developed a relationship of trust and discovered, of course, that he had spent a lot of his prison time reading the same books that we had: Bakunin, Nietzsche, Hegel, Marx. Here was a guy who took the classic self-improvement program in prison many steps further in terms of the depth of study and the radicalism. He was quick, curious, clever, funny. This was really exciting. After a week or two, things moved quickly. I said, "I think we should write your memoir."

He didn't want to do that. He said, "My story is horrible." He was really reluctant to do it. We had no idea why, because why wouldn't you want to tell your story? He said, "It was what I did to survive. Plus, I'm not a writer and I won't do any of the writing."

We said, "We'll write it. We'll record tapes." Back then that was done on a reel-to-reel machine.

Jimmy had to be stoned and/or drunk to do it. It was really painful, but we sat down, and with very little prompting from us he recorded about thirty hours of material. It covered his life from age nine when he burned down his elementary school to the present. The elementary school coach had taken a leather jacket from him. To get back at the coach, he went to the coach's office and threw a lighted match with a flammable cloth through a broken glass window and set the school on fire. I don't know how much of it burned, but part of it did.

One of the most interesting things about prison back then was that before there was so much street slang, which we have now, hip-hop and rap slang, prison slang was extremely different from the shit everyone else on the street said. The oral culture was very strong there. And one of the ways it would manifest itself would be that these guys would be locked up for some infraction in solitary. And there were specifically designated liars, or storytellers. These were guys who told stories that were incredibly vivid and lucid, they were real entertainers. To egg them on, the other prisoners would yell down the hall, "Hey, Smitty tell us a lie." And then he would say some fantastic shit. They would say, "Oh, you're lying. Don't lie like that." Of course he was lying, but Smitty, or whoever was designated, would tell these incredibly detailed tales.

We managed to get Jimmy to tell his whole story, and a lot of it was tough to hear. He talked about a couple of murders that we didn't put in the book, that he was never charged with, that happened in jail, where he was in fights and people were killed. It was brutal beyond belief. One of the reviews of the book said this was the most relentless and honest account of evil in an autobiography they had ever read. I really feel that's a fairly accurate statement because Jimmy didn't really blame the system, although the system created the situation, but he accepted responsibility for doing certain things that were choices.

When Jimmy was in and out of prison in 1970 and '71, he ran with the Black Panthers. He was actually one of Huey Newton's bodyguards and he was involved in that ideology, although he had his own suspicions, but it was the only game in town really. He'd read the standard leftist catechism and was somewhat taken by that. When we met him, we spent a lot of time going over why we thought that didn't work. Because he was a free spirit and wasn't really into Panther ideas simply to be part of an organization, but because he saw the systematic evils of the system, he was willing to abandon those ideas quickly.

He liked The Decline and Fall of the Spectacle-Commodity Economy pamphlet by the Situationists. That was an incredibly polarizing tool based on the experience of the 1965 Watts Riots. It really spoke to Jimmy because he grew up in Watts. He was in jail when the riots happened, but he understood that was a very powerful moment, and nobody else had things like that pamphlet to offer. It wasn't really a battle. It was a process that we went through with him. We would have done the book anyway, but it made it easier.

He narrated a section where he talked about George Jackson, and this was one of the most scandalous parts of the book. He had been completely lionized, mostly by whites, as a superman, a hero who could do no harm. And yet in the book he's presented in the beginning, because he goes through an evolution like everybody else, as a thug. When someone took a weight off his pile, he tried to kill him by biting his jugular vein on the yard. This is not the behavior of an altruistic radical. It's the behavior of a guy who has had a horrible life and it's an eye for an eye, a tooth for a tooth. We put that detail in the book. We put other details that were similar. And, of course, we talked about his evolution. Jimmy and George were in the same cell for months. Jimmy's honesty made the book unacceptable at that time to the liberal establishment. And the way that manifested itself was none of the liberal agents who had done similar material would touch Bad. They never said why, but we knew, because it was a book with real commercial possibilities. Bad undercut their ideology and showed them to be poseurs.
And then everything changed.

I got a phone call about six in the morning from Joan Hammer, and she said, "The worst has happened. Jimmy's dead." It was a huge shock to me.

I didn't really know what to do or think at that moment. It turned out that he had been killed by the Black Panthers, and this is one of the clearest cases of a political assassination being traced back to its origin, because the two guys who killed him jumped out of the bushes with sawed-off shotguns and slaughtered him in classic gangland style and then drove off. They went south on Highway 101 from San Jose in a car that people had seen, and they were caught. They were card-carrying members of the Black Panther Party and they'd been keeping their receipts. It was obviously a contract killing. In California, if you are caught and convicted of a contract killing, there's no parole. I assume they're still in jail. That would be forty years later, they're still in prison. It's either you are executed or you're in life in prison for a contract killing.

Then of course, the question is why did Huey Newton order the killing? There were three theories of why Jimmy was killed. One was that he was stealing money from the Angela Davis defense fund. Another one was that he killed a Black Panther member named Fred Bennett in the mountains of Santa Cruz. That did happen. Bennett was killed. And this could have been a way to get rid of his killer because they didn't want that coming back to the organization. And the third theory was that it was a classic COINTELPRO-manipulated hit. COINTELPRO was the J. Edgar Hoover–designed counterintelligence program to infiltrate various leftist groups, from pacifist groups like Martin Luther King's Freedom Marchers all the way to the most radical Marxist groups. So many of these groups had members who were FBI agents, and from within, they could spread what was called a "rat jacket" or a "dirty jacket." The word jacket in this context meant reputation, so it was about slandering somebody and then convincing others that it was true.

In any case, it was clear that the killing had been ordered by Newton, because there would have been no other reason for it to happen. Jimmy had been very close to him, and he gave us some interesting detail about his life, which we included in the book. For example, Newton was called "The Emperor" by the members of the Panthers, and he had various drug addictions, as well as a three-foot cocaine mirror which he used as he drove around in the back of his Lincoln Continental. A lot of cocaine going on there. And big surprise—tragedy happened.

Jimmy used to say, "I'm not going to live more than two more years," but he never said why. He was one of those guys who had been involved in so many murders and counter-murders in jail. People should remember this was a very heavy time. Lots of people were being killed in and out of the Black Panthers. Many, many deaths. A lot of paranoia and everyone was armed. On the white side, nothing. We didn't have anything to do with that. Between 1970 and 1976 dozens of Black Panthers were killed. In a way, Jimmy just fell during wartime, in the line of fire.

A couple of days after he died, there was a wake for him at the Hammer home. It brought together the San Jose liberal crowd, guys just out of prison, and the Venceremos Brigade. It was a very eclectic group and this was a very elegant house. Everyone was obviously totally devastated. After about five minutes into the first eulogy, delivered by Phil, who'd been to Cuba, suddenly all these gunshots rang out very close, hundreds of rounds, and we're thinking, "Oh God, we're all going to die. They've come to kill us." Everyone hit the floor and the continuous gunshots went on for two minutes. Finally they stopped, and Phil got up the courage to look out the window, but he didn't see anybody there.

What the hell? Then we started smelling smoke and we kept hearing the snap crackle of a fire. What happened was that Dan and I, about an hour before the party, had been asked to burn a bunch of milk cartons in the fireplace to get rid of them. Back then you put your paper trash in the fireplace, but these milk cartons were covered with wax and got really hot. The fire went out an hour before the party, but there was a hole in the chimney and some sparks escaped through the eaves and into the attic. Jimmy had slept up there with a .45-caliber pistol under his pillow as well as a few hundred rounds of ammunition, and the rounds all went off and blew a hole in the roof. In retrospect we thought this was cool because it was like he was sending himself off. It was the ghost of Jimmy giving himself a twenty-one-gun salute.

The party went on. The fire department came, and they put the fire out, but they were really respectful. Jimmy had made friends with a lot of people; he was such an athlete that he kind of cut through their fears—plus he and Betsy had just had a baby, he was a father, he had a job, he was working in construction. He had given up his old life. I'm sure he would never have gone back to the old ways.

There was one story that made me think twice. We were big martial arts fans. We loved Kurosawa. We had just finished taping Jimmy, and to celebrate we went to San Francisco. There was a movie theater called the Clay near the corner of Fillmore and California Street, and we went to see Yojimbo, one of the great Kurosawa Samurai films. Jimmy had one of those old Toyota land cruisers that looked exactly like the original range rover or jeep. It was very rugged. We got in the car, we parked right in front of the theater, and right to the left of the theater was the Bank of America. Jimmy opened up the glove compartment and there was his pistol. He said, in the spirit of the Kurosawa movie, "Would you guys come in with me and rob this bank?" He pulled the pistol out and said, "Because frankly, I've got nothing to lose. All you guys have to do is hold the bag and I'll do the rest." I didn't know if he was just joking, fucking with us, or calling our bluff, but if we had said yes, he would have done it. This is the kind of guy he was.

We said, "Well frankly, don't you want to finish the book?" We weren't prepared to do this. We were right in the heart of San Francisco, they could scramble cops really quickly. But there was still this kind of pull toward that hood life for Jimmy because he had robbed dozens of banks and gotten away with it.

We put the book aside for a while as we didn't have an agent. Nobody ever said that Jimmy was lying about George, because he hadn't made up anything. They just didn't want it published. Eventually, through a series of literary connections, we were introduced to a maverick in publishing called Herman Graf. He was a very offbeat, classic New Yorker who had worked as the sales director for Grove Press, the most avant-garde publishing company in the United States, which had published Malcolm X, Samuel Beckett, Frantz Fanon, Jean Genet, William Burroughs, Henry Miller, Eugene Ionesco, Octavio Paz, the Marquis de Sade, Marguerite Duras, and countless others. They were a hugely successful publishing company run by a crazy speed freak, a Jewish guy called Barney Rosset. In fact, Herman Graf was the guy who eventually found A Confederacy of Dunces by John Kennedy Toole, who had committed suicide in 1969, on the junk pile at the University of Louisiana and paid $3,000 for the book, which went on to be a huge success, critically and financially in the early 1980s. He had a great eye for the offbeat. He was eventually fired three times by Barney Rosset, and the last time he was axed, Rosse said, "Don't worry, Herman, it's only personal!" Herman started his own imprint called Whirlwind Press, and when we met him he said, "This is a fabulous book." He made us change a bunch of names of the prison officials for fear of libel suits. In the book we were explicit—for example, on such and such a day, the prison officials brought in the Nazis, the Aryan Brotherhood, and said, "If the Blacks start a fight and then retreat, we'll kill this white con." We had that kind of detail in the book.

This was in 1975. We went to France to try and publish. We thought we'd go this classic route, like Henry Miller or Robert Frank. No one wanted to publish us in America, but the French would get it. We met with some people, and they thought it could work there, but we should go back and try America one more time. It was later published in France and went through ten printings and five editions. It was a mini bestseller in France, so it turned out to have that kind of European cache after all. Herman had said he would publish the book, but he needed a distributor. The book was going to be a mass market paperback original which, in that era, meant that it was going to be sold in every drugstore, every bus station, every supermarket, every airport in the country. More cheap books were sold outside of bookstores through that method. Herman said, "Dell is the best and the biggest and I'll get them to do this book. I'll print 130,000 copies and we'll take the world by storm." We thought, great.

Then the book came out and we got a copy, but something totally weird had happened. The Dell editors had not read the book before they agreed to publish it, and they hadn't really known what was in it. At the last minute before it came out, the same kind of white liberals as the agents who had read the book and freaked out, read it at Dell and got scared—they basically decided they really didn't want to be associated with this book. They had signed a contract, so they would be sued if they did nothing, but could they sabotage our book? Was there a way to make sure that nobody really read Bad? What they did was, they disowned Bad by making it impossible to order, that is they didn't give it an ISBN number. At the last minute they pulled the copyright p that they had that was typeset and substituted a typewriter-generated title page. Not only did they not give it an ISBN number, they didn't list it in their catalogue. We said to Herman, "You have a lawsuit here. These guys have destroyed this book. It could have been a bestseller." He refused because he said they were too powerful. The book was sabotaged by the publisher.

Bad was also translated into German, and there was a Spanish edition, but essentially it had success in France. It is still an upsetting book in many ways. I think it still has legs. It has been more or less continuously in print since 1975. And as far as Jimmy's legacy, looking back, like he said, there was an extreme wave of violence, a lot of it fairly nonsensical, that happened during that period. In the end he tried to escape it, but he didn't make it.

After Jimmy was killed in the summer of 1972, I decided, along with my girlfriend, that we should split town, because at that point we had cowritten a critique of the Black Panthers and we didn't really know if this critique had gotten back to them. My girlfriend and I moved from San Francisco to Santa Cruz, which was actually closer to where Jimmy had been killed. We moved into a boardinghouse that was owned by a friend of Joan's. In this period I rediscovered my passion for food. I took over the cooking at the boardinghouse, where lentil soup was on the menu every night. At a certain point I said I'm not going to complain. I asked Dorothy, the landlady, "Can I cook for the fifteen surfers and students who are in the boardinghouse?" The only cookbook in her library was this very cryptic, comprehensive dictionary of French cooking called Larousse Gastronomique. I began making very elaborate five-course French meals with poached fish in cream sauce, bouillabaisse, and stuffed squid for $2 a person in ingredients. Dorothy was very cheap, but she loved the meals and would invite her friends over. I remember one day I was in the kitchen cooking and two African-Americans came to the door and I bolted in terror. I ran away. I thought they were there to kill me. It turned out they were the Goodwill thrift store guys who'd come to pick up a piece of furniture. Four months later Dan and I were back in Paris.

Six

I was talking with a French Situationist friend, Pierre, who spent his twenties and thirties in the Situationist milieu in Paris in the seventies and eighties. He said the Situationists managed to maintain a kind of splendid isolation, and aside from going out in the streets in '68, they had their own universe, they had their own cafés, their own bars, their own world. They weren't on the news. They weren't media personalities. They became the focus of the media, but they never cultivated that. They had this imaginary world which you could see in the early Debord films of the late fiftiess and early sixties where they talked about living in this bohemian universe that they constructed. They made forays into the world at large, but they were essentially in this hidden universe that they managed to maintain despite all the popularity that they achieved.

Of course, we in California were victims of the era in a lot of ways, and this marks the time when, even though we thought of ourselves as anti-spectators, in some ways we played more of a spectator's role than we realized at the time. Not to say spectators in the sense of "spectators of the spectacle," but observers of our own lives rather than makers of our lives. We were aware of this. We were aware that we were at an existential crisis point. We decided to do what other generations of American bohemians have done over the centuries, and what we had done previously in 1970. We went to Paris.

One of the reasons we returned was because in 1970 we had met a

French radical and his partner, Roger Gregoire and Linda Lanphear, in San Francisco. They had collaborated with the author/activist Fredy Perlman, because Roger had been at Kalamazoo, where Perlman, among other things, had stirred controversy as a professor at Western Michigan University for allowing students to grade themselves. Roger had met Perlman and Linda there, and they worked on a text that became quite well known, called The Worker Student Action Committee, which was a really interesting first-person account of what happened in '68 from a radical but not doctrinaire Situationist point of view. Roger invited us to come to France. He was living in a seventh-floor walk-up in the 13th Arrondisement at Place D'Italie. It was a pretty ordinary workers' neighborhood. No tourism there. You went to the farmers market in the square twice a week and got a chicken with the feathers on it, brought it back home, and plucked it. In their tiny apartment there were five or six of us there at times. The shower was a plastic tub suspended on pegs over the toilet. The kitchen was tiny, but that didn't stop us from making elaborate meals. We were young and it worked out perfectly. If it was really crowded, we would go across the street to the hotel that was $3 a night and stay in what was essentially flophouse for traveling salesmen.

Roger had been totally involved in '68. He had great stories and you can refer to that text and others for them. He introduced us to his collaborator, Jean-Pierre Voyer, who would play a huge role in my life and in many ways in the post-Situationist world. At that time there were literally hundreds, if not thousands, of what were called Pro-Situs, meaning Situationist followers, all battling for the title of who was the least Pro-Situ, if that makes sense. No one wanted to be just an observer or a spectator. They all wanted to come up with an idea of how to criticize what had happened in the SI, but Debord made that very difficult in a way, because he didn't leave a theoretical opening. He said that the "epic" alone created the spectators, the Pro-Situ. There was nothing in the ideas of the Situationists that was responsible for this theoretical vacuum, this failure of the movement to achieve its goals. There was no way for an exit point and a new way out of the situation. Debord disowned all of that. If you look at what he wrote, he said it was the fault of the "epic" because the world is full of spectators, passive consumers of everything. Why not of the SI's theory? Why couldn't there be passive consumers of the Situationist movement itself, especially since it wasn't obvious what to do next? After '68 things seemed to have gone back to semi-normal, but it wasn't completely normal. We were young and naïve, and we hadn't really realized that the world had changed. We didn't understand that the system had been deeply threatened by the events of the 1960s and had taken very seriously the possibility that if it didn't make profound changes in the way the world was run, in the way products were developed and sold, and in the way ideologies were manipulated, the old world and its power brokers could fall.

We can debate how much of this was consciously planned and how much of it was simply the market evolving to survive. And of course, television took off, and previously there had been the artificial constraint of having four or five channels, and a few radio stations. And the capitalists knew they were leaving a lot of money on the table because they were leaving people out. I like the Adam Curtis's documentary Century of the Self because I was thinking that the hippies and the Leftists—which encompassed, in various mutations, pretty much all of the baby boom generation who were oppositional—both groups were really ascetic. We lived on nothing. We didn't buy anything. We bought the essentials. We weren't into clothing. We bought a few records, and we bought a few books. The world of consumerism could not go on with its expansion plans with people like us being the lead force, because we didn't buy enough. We didn't spend enough money and we didn't care about working. None of us thought we should have a career, because the revolution was going to end capitalism. That was to be our retirement plan. This wasn't a widely shared idea in the culture at large, but it was shared among enough people that we weren't alone in that concept. The baby boom generation had to be taught to consume. They had to learn these behaviors. Our parents were pretty good consumers, but we had gone through such a radical break with that gluttonous lifestyle, that the whole generation had to be retaught to consume but on a different model than our parents. I like Adam Curtis's idea about creating the needy self. I remember at that time I would encounter people who I thought were relatively intelligent and interesting and they would say things like "I really like est" or "I really like Scientology." Those were some of the ways that people learned that the self was good, that desire was important, that the individual ego and satisfying it were really noble pursuits. One of the things that you learn from seeing Curtis's documentary, and that I also remember from the period, is that our parents were too obedient, they were too passive, and they were too accepting. There was a kind of dead end with them. They would consume, but they weren't contributing enough back. There was no learning, no feedback. There was no critical element. And the universe we're living in now is all about individuals creating themselves as a commodity more than just buying products. Our parents fought World War II, and this was their reward: the right to remain silent.

In France a lot of people were talking about whether we were living in the society of Situationism with the leaders pretending to understand the spectacle or whether the society needed to be modified in some other way. There was really very little wholesale radical reexamination of basic concepts of the spectacle. Jean-Pierre came along after writing an almost humorous book, an encyclopedia of the Situationists, titled Situationist International. He had the names and reasons for the exclusion of all Situationists, and a hilarious list of people—an index—of everyone who had been insulted by the SI. Jean-Pierre was a restless spirit, and to give you an idea of the difference between him and Debord, who actually thought of JP as his successor, this was a guy who in an earlier stage had met Jean Paul Sartre and had shown such an understanding of existentialism that, according to Roger, he was, at least for a while, Sartre's personal secretary. Extremely bright guy; even in France where there are so many precocious, clever philosophers, he stood out on another level.

The aforementioned Pierre was at Guy Debord's apartment in 1971, so Pierre would have been twenty-three or twenty-four, and JP and Debord older by a few years. They were having a discussion about whether the unconscious exists. Debord said of course it does, because his schooling was in surrealism, and the unconscious was a powerful force there—surrealists believe they can tap it, but they can never truly dominate it. And Jean-Pierre said, "Bullshit. What's really going on here is that this is a limit forced upon us by a traditional constraint and it's not the case." Very soon after that he wrote a text addressing this issue that is available in the book called *It's Crazy How Many Things Don't Exist*, published by Little Black Cart and also separately in a translation from Ken Knabb. In it he said character, meaning neurosis, is the absence of theory. Pierre said that at that moment with the two of them in the apartment he could see the difference between Debord and Jean-Pierre, because although Debord was charming and historical, he really was in a way accepting of certain conventions, and Jean Pierre was constantly challenging them.

Pierre ended up working with JP for fifteen years. Jean-Pierre published a book right around that point called The Science Of Publicity, which unfortunately has been translated poorly in underground circles and never published in English. That was his first attempt to go beyond the spectacle while using it. He wasn't ready to break with the concept of the spectacle yet, but he talked for the first time about the idea that the reason that so many people had spent so much time willingly going along with the market and commodities was because in the commodity there is a community, which is false and untrue, but a community nonetheless, a general, universal source of wealth, and of communication. There's a dialectical meaning to this. Whereas if you look at the society of the spectacle, you only see misery. You see alienation. You don't see humanity in the spectacle, you see inhumanity, and then eventually if we revolt, in the act of revolt we discover that humanity. This is a traditional Hegelian approach applied to the modern context.

 We were highly influenced by the JP text Reich: How to Use. We decided that we were going to translate that in our own American way into an advertisement for ourselves. We were incorporating this new "Century of the Self" approach, but we tried to do it in a way that was both self-deprecating and humorous. This was before personal ads existed. This was before Craigslist. The only personal ads were sex ads in the Berkeley Barb, the Los Angeles Free Press, and other newspapers. You went to these things like est or Scientology to meet people as much as anything else, but you weren't freelancing publicly looking for companionship. We decided to freelance. We came up with this idea of doing a poster between '72 and '73. The poster was called We're Tired of Playing with Ourselves, and this was a poster with our photos on it. Before that, I can't remember anything that we did that had our pictures. What we did wasn't personal in that way. The Situationist stance had always had a glacial voice like in the film Society of the Spectacle, the all-knowing genius theorist explains it all to you. We were thinking, "What if we showed some vulnerability?"

 We hadn't really been involved actively in these groups such as Esalen, and encounter groups, and ego psychology, and all these seminars. That had just blossomed at this point. We knew about it, but we thought it was counterrevolutionary and bourgeois. We tried to concoct our own version of this on our own terms, which I think was pretty original in a way. It was completely out of nowhere as far as most people were concerned. But this bridge created by Jean-Pierre's text allowed us to do the American version. We produced a poster that was seventeen by twenty-two inches, a large photo slightly in outline, but you could still recognize us, and there was a critique of our complacent yuppie life. And this was before the word yuppie existed. We said, "We were like you. We were cynical, smug. We read Dashiell Hammett, we made fun of the San Francisco Chronicle. We went to the nice restaurants." Before there was even that kind of epicurean movement or food consciousness, it was San Francisco dining. We didn't have much money, but it didn't take much. We were living this kind of yuppie or bourgeoise bohemian life. We said that the society kept us from meeting, it was their goal, which was and is true. Isolation. We see that now with the automobile, television, Facebook, the whole thing. We were saying that was already happening to us. And we didn't like it. We wanted to reach out to people. And we proposed that people get in touch with us. Back then it was all done through a post office box. We didn't give out our phone numbers. We were restricted to written communication, which was interesting because it took a lot of work and you had to consider things, you didn't rush out and do things. It had to matter to you to make the effort. You couldn't just blurt things out. We put up the posters on the walls of Berkeley and San Francisco with wheat paste, the standard stuff for public billboards and posters then, but we weren't competing with ads and event announcements, as it wasn't so crowded where we put ours up. We put them in the middle of Telegraph Avenue, and on the windows of buildings and storefronts. We didn't really care if they found us. We put up maybe four hundred of these posters.

    A week later we went to the PO box and we couldn't even open it because there were so many letters. It was five or six hundred responses. There was every kind of approach, from "Let's have a sex party" to "I'm insane, can we talk?" to "You want to start a business?" One of the biggest regrets in my life is that I moved so many times and I was so cavalier I didn't keep the letters. I think they would still be valuable in a way. We attracted the attention of one of the founders of the Yippie party. There was Abbie Hoffman, there was Stew Albert, who disappeared after running for mayor of Berkeley. And then there was a guy called Paul Krassner, who survived until just recently, and he had a publication that was very popular then called the Realist. He was part of the Rolling Stone crowd, but he was famous because he put a picture of Lyndon Johnson, naked, fucking John Kennedy's neck wound on the cover of his publication. That was so scatological at that time—and he was basically saying Johnson had something to do with the JFK assassination. He was a really radical guy and completely independent. The Realist had a pretty big circulation and it was on all the newsstands. Krassner offered us the possibility of editing an entire issue of the Realist. Being such snobs, we said no thanks. We were just too cool for that. And I really regret that because I think we were on to something. It's not like we could have made a career of it, but there was something that was going on there. We had tapped a vein and we were criticizing implicitly all this early stage egoism stuff that was going on.

 Next year we went back to France again, and we had the posters with us. We met Jean-Pierre in his tiny garret apartment in the Latin Quarter. We showed him the poster and he got so excited. He started screaming and yelling and we went down to the street. He was yelling, "I love the Americans!" He jumped from car to car, landing on the roofs of the vehicles. You can actually crush the roof of a car if you land on the top right. He was in ecstasy. He could never have done what we did. As radical as he was, for him it was all

about getting the ideas right. It wasn't about experimenting with the means of communication. They kept saying to us "We're a team!" They were in some ways diminishing our intellectual capacity, saying in essence, "Right, you guys know how to communicate and what we know is how to think and write." That really made Jean-Pierre happy, that he'd found collaborators. It's not like he'd figured he could do it all, but he hadn't been looking for new ideas, it was all in his head pretty much. He kept going for years, one of those people who has the plan all laid out. But it was also a matter of executing it right. We were ideal collaborators for him.

Just to give you an idea of Jean-Pierre's character—a true ebullient spirit—unlike the very cool Situationists or Sartre. On my fiftieth birthday I came to Paris to celebrate, and he took us, my ex-wife Terrel and I, to a restaurant that had one of the largest cellars in France, and he had an encyclopedic understanding of French wine. He started ordering, and the wine got older and older; eventually it was sixty years old. He was working in a modest job, in his own software company, and he was making something like six grand a month, an average amount for that kind of job. The wine bill was one month's salary, and he just laughed and paid it, and I was crying. I was so moved by that. I didn't expect anything like that, but for him it was easy come, easy go. I thought this guy really understood the gift, he really did. It didn't even occur to him not to do that.

Coming back to America, compared to the streets and cafés of Paris, we were in the shadows, but still in the game. We were still, in our way, contributing to something really interesting, an international collaboration. Even if wasn't the SI, which at its height in the mid sixties had five or six national sections and a highly influential international journal, we had this Berkeley/Paris access. That was an important meeting ground for many other people too, including filmmakers, philosophers, and historians. They were many other people who saw that connection and used it. It makes sense and it's still alive today. Berkeley is the most French place in the United States in a lot of different ways even though people make fun of it.

We had an extended milieu. There were people who had been involved in Point Blank, people who had been involved in Contradiction, and we were all still hanging out. This is '73, '74. If you look at what happened in those years, there are a lot of contradictory tendencies all swirling and evolving in a political sense. The United States had basically lost the war in Vietnam. The streets were littered just as they are now, only more so, with heroin-addicted veterans, maimed guys, amputees. The failure of our escapade in Asia was highly visible. Despite America denying that we had lost the war to a superior military strategy, and army, and approach, it was apparent that the war had been a total defeat. That denial goes on to this day, but clearly General Giap, the head of the NVA (North Vietnamese Army), beat General Westmoreland at his own game, no matter what anybody says. There was this dark cloud, this sadness hanging over America at the time. We were beginning to realize that we'd lost our war too, but at the same time, the majority of the baby boom generation, who had never shared the view that radical social change was necessary, were thinking they'd done great because they had helped end the war. They were thinking as a generation, "We've done our job, we can do whatever we want. We can enter the workplace, we can enter the market."

What we were left with was Patty Hearst being kidnapped by the SLA. We're thinking, "How do we even say anything about this? This is so ridiculous." It gave a lot of weight to the idea that everything was going to become a spectacle, because you had this huge media circus over no ideas at all, it was all completely superficial and inconsequential. This was a kick in the face to us at that point. What that translated into was a lot of hand-wringing and some Pro-Situ pamphlet writing trying to figure out what went wrong. There was the introduction a year or two later from Paris of a critique of the Situationist milieu as being misogynist, although that word wasn't used. Arms and the Woman was translated by Ken Knabb.

The SI and Pro Situ milieu was in fact misogynist. I knew a lot of feminists who had incisive things to say, and I paid attention to their anger because I realized this was a profound historical problem. Recently I watched part of the Society of the Spectacle and realized that in nearly all the images of women in the film, they are naked or in bikinis. There was an exhibit called The Bay Area's Situationists at the Pro Arts Gallery in Oakland recently, along with a screening of Ken's translation of the film. Women are sex objects in these SI films; it goes on and on. In the earlier films there were pictures of Michelle Bernstein and other participants in the Paris scene who were actively involved in the production process as well, but they were the obvious exception.

There was a lot of fighting and there were a lot of relationships breaking up over this issue. The French, since they were French, did write something here and there. They called the hierarchical relationship at SI "Behindism." People asked me this over and over again: "Was this milieu different from other radical leftist scenes?" There were some women involved in SDS and in all these other groups, but the ratio was typical of what you'd expect. I'm not proud of that legacy. There wasn't any more honest, fundamental criticism or change compared to the outside world. We, in some sense, simply copied the world.

By 1975 our group had pretty much disbanded. I had created a journal with one of the founders of Point Blank, Chris Shutes, that came out in 1974, called Implications. We were reduced to writing lengthy articles about people who fetishized personal transformation over social revolt. I kept using my theoretical chops almost out of instinct. We were doing something very sectarian, even delusional in a way. By that point, fortunately, the world outside continued, and there were revolts in various places. There were insurrections in Northern Italy, revolts in Poland, riots in South Africa. We realized that we had to keep focusing on that. We started writing commentaries and publishing essays and leaflets on those events. We were pulled out of ourselves. And at the same time, unbeknownst to us, Jean-Pierre was developing a very radical critique of the SI, of Marxism, and of the economy, which was published in 1976. I read it in French, and it went completely over my head because it was a really complicated, and it took twenty years for the world to catch up. We are publishing that work shortly through Little Black Cart. It's called An Inquiry into the Nature and Causes of the Misery of People, a takeoff on the Adam Smith title.

Essentially Jean-Pierre said that the commodity is not material, that the economy doesn't exist, meaning the economy exists only in the minds of our rulers. There's no such thing as an economy that acts autonomously. There is the commodity and there is money, capital, that dominate us. But the idea of the economy per se, which is a system separate from the market, a material force outside of what people can control—as when people say "the economy is going to turn on us"—is false. It's similar to the idea of the spectacle in the sense that it's an abstraction. The way Jean-Pierre says it most clearly is: "Religion exists, God doesn't. The economy doesn't exist, but the market does." As with God, you have this abstract, unknowable power that dominates us. No matter what we do, it will be there as an irrational force to determine our lives. That's very similar to the idea of the spectacle, which has a thousand different faces and it's contradictory. The economy has a similar role. It has a thousand different faces and it is all-powerful, escaping the control of human beings. In a way it always will be beyond control.

Jean-Pierre sees the dominant force in society being the commodity that we invest with our entire humanity. We grant it the power to speak profound truths. The other side, the truly human side, is conversation, dialogue, which makes perfect sense. He calls it bavardage, or chitchat. But profound chitchat. Forget about the economy. Commodities are talking, commodities are living, they're acting for us. They're literally acting on our behalf and we carry them around. He calls people commodity porters, commodity mules. We are the servants of commodities. It's everywhere. It's not simply advertising. It's the language that we hear, what we see, what we know. This sound that we hear is commodities talking to each other, and we're listening. In the same way he says that because we aren't speaking for ourselves, the spectacle speaks, the spectacle exists. He flips it on its head. But what he's saying, more importantly than simply our masters are our masters is that we are mastered by commodities. And, of course, those commodities are in the service of power, but in a real immediate way, we are the servants of those commodities. He's saying because we don't speak, because we are mute, because slaves actually don't control their lives, in the void of our silence, the blah, blah, blah, the spectacle is there, and that it's simply just filler, noise. We think something is being said inside the spectacle, but it is that noise, the noise of machines talking to each other, so there is not a moment of silence.

What is really exciting about that is that you then don't spend that much time figuring out the ins and outs of every specific ideology, or every specific commodity message, or every specific intellectual trend. It's all nonsense essentially. Compared to what we really have to say, it's gibberish. JP is saying then that the spectacle is the result of our alienation, not the cause of it. An example is from '68 when the crisis took place and the workers and the students were in the streets for three weeks and at a certain point the official press went relatively silent. They were rendered almost speechless. They had nothing to say because there was another dialogue taking place—the dialogue of spectacle—and the demonstrators and workers didn't feel like if they intruded, if they yelled, they would be listened to, and they weren't.

We have, for example, in our own time a surreal event when the World Trade Center was attacked and what followed was the attack on the twin towers re-running over and over again with no narrative or analysis—just that image showing as spectacle—because there can't be "nothing." I've never met a single person who has read the Society of the Spectacle who can actually do more than repeat what it says. I've never met somebody who has made any improvements. There isn't another person that takes that book further.

One of the things that was told to me was that Jean-Pierre wrote a letter a day for three years criticizing Bernard-Henri Lévy, and sent each one to him, a really insulting letter. He also wrote letters criticizing Debord and his publishing partner, Gérard Lebovici. Together they had a publishing company named Champs Libre in the seventies, and it was the house organ for Debord and the SI in a lot of ways. He got to pick most of the books. Jean-Pierre was very self-critical. He started with the concept of publicity and he eventually came up with the idea of communication, which I think is a very approachable and a much more easily understandable concept. He was constantly renewing his theoretical perspective.

Seven

I was just saying to Aragorn, now deceased, the founder and editor of Little Black Cart, an anarchist publishing collective, that until 1977 when I was in my late twenties I was in an extended nursery school version of the Situationist milieu. Even though the world had changed and we weren't activists in the same way. We had a social routine and a network where we all hung out together that was based on this nostalgia for another time, but also based on failure and on trying to figure out if there was a way to get back to that sensibility, that feeling, that level of camaraderie that wasn't going to return. We began to realize that it was never coming back. It was hard to give up that idea.

Life intruded, and I had what I would describe as a male nesting instinct. I met and became involved with a woman who was a bohemian artist, Terrel Seltzer. She ran around Telegraph Avenue wearing a red vinyl jumpsuit in the Andy Warhol style, very cool, really short hair. Someone came up to her once and said, "Are you David Bowie or David Bowie's girlfriend?" It was that polymorphous look. She was working in a dress store called Yarmo where the European-style women in Berkeley worked. If you wanted to meet a non-hippie woman, this is where you went. Terrel was an aspiring video maker.

Quickly, she got pregnant. We had a kid in 1978. We were the first in our group to have one, and we had the idea that we were going to keep separate apartments and not live together, and raise the kid in this more European, free-form style. Her roommate was an established, and still well-known academic in feminist film studies, a critic named Constance Penley. She and two other women published a magazine called Camera Obscura, and they were enthusiastic champions of the French structuralists and women filmmakers, and all very pro-Godard and pro-SI.

At that time there was an amorphous scene centered around the California cuisine progenitor Chez Panisse, that very innovative restaurant, which I later became involved with through the food movement. It was a mixture of European filmmakers, the best ones who were coming to the Pacific Film Archive run at that point by Tom Luddy, who later started the Telluride Film Festival and worked with Francis Coppola. All these filmmakers would visit—Rainer Fassbinder, Barbet Schroeder, Werner Herzog, Wim Wenders, Jean-Luc Godard. Martin Scorsese came to use the film archive with Liza Minnelli. It was a very salon atmosphere. Francis Coppola was about to release Apocalypse Now, and he was very concerned that the intelligentsia like his movie. He decided to bribe Constance Penley. She became his girlfriend. Francis came over to Terrel and Connie's humble apartment in the Berkeley Hills above the football stadium and slept on the foam pad on the floor and talked about movies. He gave us a lot of presents: cases of wine, the use of a car, and most lavishly, an office for Camera Obscura in the American Zoetrope building, one of the most beautiful buildings in North Beach, an office Terrel kept for decades.

here was a wild, unpredictable, mix going on. That was very seductive in a different way than Situationist ideas. Tom Luddy somehow figured out that I was political, and he was extremely manic, as everyone said, before he got his lithium medication. One night he and I and Connie walked around North Beach at four in the morning, and he explained that he already had a lot of space for editing and making films, and now he was going to take over the neighborhood and make me his political minister. Given what was happening, this was an appealing idea. It was the power of money, and he was a very narcissistic kind of guy who loved to wield it.

I saw that I had to do other things to make a living. I had been working in a laborers union setting up trade show booths, and at one of the shows, the American Booksellers Association Convention, Bad was on display. I had an epiphany. I was a writer, I could get paid to create books. Because I had been involved as a commercial fisherman in the Monterey Bay, I thought I was going to find a way to write something about my experience, write books that would be as distant as possible from Situationist theory to avoid any confusion. I wanted to draw a clear line. I thought, as a joke, what's the least political subject? Food. Food writing was about living like a European. It was about being a gourmet, an epicurean, living the good life, but it didn't have a critique of the commodification of food, of pollution, of miserable working conditions in kitchens. None of that was present. We had all been to Europe, and in reaction to how truly horrible American food was at that moment, we saw the alternative of living better, eating better, as a lifestyle choice. I decided to write cookbooks as a way to make a living, and then I would keep doing theory in a separate space.

I wrote a book about squid and it was published by a small press. Back then, it's worth noting, was the high point of small press publishing. Especially in the Bay Area you had a lot of small publishers who were publishing, not necessarily radical books, but books on new ideas. And if you as a publisher found an author who had a good idea and you could find commissioned sales reps to represent you, they would find hundreds of bookstores to carry the books, from the chains down to the smallest neighborhood shops. There were a lot of channels to distribute books, so you could actually sell as many or more copies of a book as a New York publisher. You could definitely compete with those publishers.

I became involved with John Harris, who had written and published The Book of Garlic. It's funny to remember that back then—the seventies and early eighties—you could not buy fresh garlic in a supermarket in America. You could only buy the powdered herb unless you went to the Chinese grocery store or the Italian markets. I approached John with a proposal for a book on squid, and after first saying no, he eventually responded, "I guess I'll publish it because squid is the garlic of the sea," meaning unpopular. He was totally uninterested unless it made sense in "John world." I became involved with writing, designing, marketing, selling, and publicizing books. The company, Aris, did a second book, an encyclopedia of Pacific Coast seafood. There were no books on West Coast seafood because all the chefs at the time focused on the Atlantic- and European-style recipes. It's hard to believe this was the case. The book became popular and I took a job with Aris in 1982.

At the same time Terrel, who had been previously married to a Chinese director called Wayne Wang, got a call from him. He had raised $20,000 in grants from the NEA and the AFI to make a movie about Chinatown. He asked her to help him work on the film, which later became Chan Is Missing. They started on this project and they never really had a formal script. It was a story about a taxicab driver who disappeared in Chinatown. The guy never existed. His character was a literary device. It was a way to explore San Francisco's Chinatown when it was still a real Chinatown, filled with fish and poultry markets, herb and tea shops, Chinese-language movie theaters, dive bars, acupuncturists, and Chinese Brotherhood halls. There were no T-shirts, no jade. It still had a bit of its mystique, with a lot of historic restaurants, dim sum parlors, laundry hanging from fire escapes, and a Chinese New Year's Parade. Wayne's film came together in 1982, the year that Terrel and I worked on a film entitled Call It Sleep.

With the small budget Wayne and Terrel made a 16mm black-and-white film, which you could do back then. They edited it and it didn't quite hold together. They decided to bring me in. Wayne said, "We have this older taxi driver in his late fifties. Great character. What about if we have you write a voice-over for him?" At that time I was reading Walter Benjamin, and I made the taxicab driver a Walter Benjamin character, musing about the existential mysteries of the city. Somehow that worked. The movie was shown at the New Directors Showcase at the New York Film Festival in October of 1982 and a miracle happened. The very powerful head film critic at the New York Times, Vincent Canby, reviewed the film. He went crazy about it and said it was one of the best movies he'd ever seen. He called it "a matchless delight." That night Wayne, who was staying at a friend's house, got two hundred phone calls from people in the industry. I got a screen credit. The film was later inducted into the National Film Registry of the Library of Congress, in 1995. It was one the very first ethnic American films. Spike Lee came three or four years later with his films. But this was a Chinese-American project. It ended up being very popular and helped Wayne and Terrel's film careers that continue to this day.

1982 was the high point of the punk scene in San Francisco. There was the Mabuhay Gardens with the Dead Kennedys and other bands, three or four years after the Sex Pistols. The reigning critical, radical, antisocial activity in the Bay Area at that point was punk, and I wanted to reach this new audience with a new message. I wrote a text to analyze, in a very Guy Debord, Von Clausewitz way, the strategic forces in society. I divided the world into six groups. To my surprise when Terrel read this, because she really hadn't been so involved in this theory, she said, "Let's make a video out of one of the sections called The

Cadre." In French the word cadre means "office worker," but it's really in fact "yuppie." It's the person who wants to have his cake and eat it too. Debord described it in 1971 as the desire to "live simultaneously the joy of submission and the thrill of refusal."

In France there were the proto yuppies. These were the despicable guys and gals who were perfectly quaffed, had that very tight suit with the shirt with the pointed collar. They read Le Monde, went to the right cafés and restaurants, knew about Godard. They had a vaguely critical idea of capitalism, but they were also incredibly ambitious in a traditional way. The word yuppie didn't exist, but the phenomenon was happening below the sociologists' radar. We were helping to identify this social type in a way, even though we didn't fully understand what was going to happen. It was all about consumerism and styles of consumption. The society was stumbling on the fact that the only way it would grow was to provide those alternative forms of consumerism called lifestyle choices. That was the key for the powers that be, as it was no longer about an individual product. They figured out they could group together commodities in a way that was much more successful because once you bought the lifestyle, you bought ten, and they didn't have to sell you each one separately. They sold themselves to you as a package, moreover a package that was always having to be updated.

We decided to make the first section of the film on The Cadre. I had five other chapters sitting on the side. Terrel was confident this was the way to launch the project. It was contemporary as it was not about leftism, or even about the spectacle per se. It was about how the commodity society was micromanaged and personalized in such a way that people would identify with their merchandising and products. The liberals or the intelligentsia wouldn't be able to say that this was about somebody else, because it included them.

Literally, we were making a critique about the people who would go to see the video, who were at the Pacific Film Archive, who were in that world. At that time independent film was in its adolescence; it was virtually nonexistent except for maybe John Cassavetes. For example, there weren't any distributors of independent films to work with Chan Is Missing other than New Yorker Films. There was no Sony Classics or others, as they came later. Fortunately, New Yorker Films wanted to distribute the movie. This was a really groundbreaking film in a lot of ways and there was a lot of ground to break.

As for Call It Sleep, it was a video. Video was all about "video art" with very little narrative. It was experimental, similar to the San Francisco school, where they were literally painting on film. There were a few documentaries, but they were mainly shown on PBS. There wasn't a whole wave of thousands of documentaries where you've got a short on purple nail polish. That just didn't exist. To actually make a video at that point was a real technical challenge also, because there was no digital editing. Everything was done on tape, and the wider the format the better the quality. There were three formats: half-inch tape, which amateurs used; three-quarter-inch tape, which was an expensive art form as it required professional-quality machines; and then there was one-inch broadcast tape. All the television work for conventional broadcast television was done in this last format, and the equipment was owned by the networks and local affiliates. Fortunately, because we were in Berkeley and because we had a relationship with David Ross, the director of the Berkeley Art Museum, who later ran the Whitney Museum, he lent us the three-quarter-inch Sony camera that they had, at no cost.

We decided to do this project in a different way than the classic Situationist style, in keeping with our intention to Americanize Situationist theory. There weren't that many models. Guy Debord was pretty much it. His

CALL IT SLEEP
A VIDEOTAPE BY ISAAC CRONIN AND TERREL SELTZER

"The Spectacle rules by ideas as well as by armies."

"Everyone is encouraged to play the roles of bureaucrat and scientist in his own home."

"The founding father of modern cinema was a Bolshevik."

"There is no difference Bolshevism and all other brands of spectacular opposition."

"The current wave of terrorism is primarily the consequence of the proletariat's refusal to be organized by the Bolsheviks."

"The new revolt is as likely to appear in a totalitarian regime like South African or China."

early films from the fifties, and Society of the Spectacle made a little later, were the collected Situationist film works. We did not write a drama, but an episodic storyline with actors and characters. Then we taped it as if we were making a short dramatic film, which people really hadn't done up to that point. We were trying to film theory differently. We weren't trying to make a parody, a satire, or a documentary. We found some amateur actors. We found some locations. We did a short film of about seventeen minutes. We found a professional actor to read voice-over, and we shot from a script that I had written where I tried to imagine condensed yuppie talk. I mixed the original theoretical text in voice-over and the dialogue that I wrote.

An example of one scene: A guy is getting out of a fancy swimming pool, and his girlfriend says, "Your food was great, Jean. Maybe you should be a chef." It's this classic thing where everyone thinks they can do everything. Everyone's a screenwriter, everyone's a chef. It fits the current moment, right? Very concentrated bits of what a yuppie would say. We finished it and started showing it around to people and they liked it. We also had titles as well as voice-over. It was kind of a dense work. There were titles spread through the film with different kinds of cadre sayings. Krishnamurti was in there, as well as Godard. It was extremely tongue-in-cheek. And that was another thing that we were concerned about because we were trying to consciously create an alternative to the very somber French style of theory. The Viénet martial arts send-up films were funny, but that was a completely different approach. We wanted it to be off-the-wall. People got really excited because I guess it was new. They knew about the SI, but the film stood on its own. At that point we thought we should make some more sections. The problem was, once again, technical. Everything was incredibly expensive. VHS and Betamax, the video recorders, had just come out, and they were thousands of dollars to purchase, and obviously we didn't have the money.

Terrel got a job with a commercial video company that had recorders. We brought a machine home and gave ourselves the weekend because her employers were out of town, and we recorded whatever we could. It made us very focused. We recorded movies: Apocalypse Now, Close Encounters of the Third Kind, Three Days of the Condor. And we had some classic films transferred, Ten Days That Shook the World, documentary footage of Castro. We were going to work backwards from the footage that we had. We had the text, but we didn't really know exactly how it was going to edit together. It was an intuitive process, like flying blind, like playing a jazz song. Was that the right show to tape? You can only record one at a time. It was a wild weekend where we hoped we would get what we needed.

We had all this footage, how the hell were we going to make a video? We heard about a group in San Francisco called the Bay Area Video Coalition, a nonprofit organization, that is still around. And they had just purchased the first time code–based, three-quarter-inch editing equipment, at a huge cost. We showed up and said, "This is what we're doing." They weren't really political. They said, "Well this is amazing. We're going to let you edit here and we're going to edit this for you—and for free!" They gave us hundreds of hours of editing. The editor donated his time. Amazing. This whole project cost us less than $1,000 out of our pockets. We paid for lunch on the set a few days. Here's where my ex-wife was really great. She knew how to edit. There's some incredible cuts going from a traveling shot of Auschwitz with somber music to an insane Kellogg's shredded wheat commercial. It seems odd, but it shows you the craziness of the world we live in. It's a brilliant jump cut. We spent months working on the film.

This was the same year that Chan Is Missing was coming out. I felt like

Eisenstein, who did all of his great stuff in his twenties. I was the same age, right? I also wrote three cookbooks and had kids in the same period. Terrel and I worked on the video and completed forty-two minutes in four parts. Then we confronted another issue. How were we going to get is seen? PBS was not going to show our video because there was so much footage that had a copyright. There were a few festivals, including the San Francisco Video Festival. We were completely odd for the festival circuit because our program was four times as long as anything else. Call It Sleep was completely different in content also. It made no sense in the context, but it found a home.

Another technical issue was that video projectors were very weak. They weren't digital. They were murky. You projected on a screen this very dark image that you couldn't read very well. It was almost out of focus. It was a three-gun lens called an Advent. They were incredibly expensive, costing about $20,000. But you still couldn't see what was being projected because it was three different colors trying to meet up. We showed the video first at the Pacific Film Archive, which was full because we had all our friends there. We knew someone who was one of the owners of the Roxy Theater in San Francisco, and we wanted to reach this street audience. He agreed to show the video. They promoted it really well. I remember it was a great night. We had the black-clad San Francisco crowd, and six hundred people came to two screenings. Then it started making the museum circuit. It was shown all over. I was asked to speak at the Chicago Art Institute. I realized that even though I didn't have an MFA I could have a career at this, explaining the Situationists the way academic hacks like McKenzie Wark do. But I knew I couldn't do it. I took On the Poverty of Student Life to heart, and I didn't imagine that I was ever going to be able to really stand there—very serious and professorial—and I never did.

Eight Q&A

What are your thoughts on the anarchist subculture both as you experienced it in the past and as it is now?

I had a very brief dash through the anarchist culture because I went from a Bolshevik to an anarchist to a Situationist in what seemed like a week. In that period everything was concentrated, everything moved really quickly. You could go through a whole political metamorphosis, if you were open to it, in a few months.

We got ahold of the anarchist texts. It was all floating around mixed in with the Situationist books and pamphlets. And we came across Anarchos, the publication Murray Bookchin put out, and a lot of it seemed impractical because he was talking about a utopian vision of integrating city and country without suppressing capitalism. He was very influenced by Lewis Mumford, the urbanist, and by Jane Jacobs, whose campaign saved Greenwich Village. An essential part of New York would have otherwise been destroyed. That was a huge deal—that they managed to hold off Robert Moses, who was going to put a freeway through the heart of lower Manhattan. He had destroyed a large part of New York with the BQE and other highways that severed neighborhoods in the Bronx and Queens. His last target was the Village. Bookchin lived on the Lower East Side. I went to his apartment. It was in a low cost housing project on Third Street. He was the key figure for us because he had some ideas and he was competing with the Situationists.

In 1969 Anarchos called a national anarchist conference. Remember that '68 had just happened. The conference was held in Black River Falls. I decided to go. It was right around the time of Woodstock, almost simultaneous with it, in August of 1969. At the conference they intended to make a critique of the bureaucracy of the Left. The thing is, even though Bookchin mentioned play as a strategy and he had a critique of daily life, he didn't really do playful things himself, he was arguing for an abstract program. He wasn't sexy, he wasn't fun. And at that point we quickly became the California Situationists. We were heading to that. This was August. We did the suicide letter a few months later and then we moved to Berkeley. It all happened really fast, so my interest in official anarchism was nothing more than a brief flirtation.

As for present day anarchists in the Bay Area I'm not really drawn to the way people live. I came from an upper-middle-class background. My father was a successful radiologist briefly. I had a spoiled youth and my family appreciated food. My father was an early gourmet. He knew about food in the 1950s. I was raised in—well I wouldn't say an aristocratic, but a classic, almost European, upper-middle-class Jewish household. My father was a great dresser. I always cared about clothes. I'm a product of my family, and I really am not at all attracted to the way people live as anarchists in this world now. We had communal group houses, but we would go around and steal only the best wine and steak. We were into luxury. We thought the Situationist idea was not that we were going to give up luxury, but that we were going to transform it. That was how I read it. There's a barrier between the way I live and have lived in this world and the anarchist scene. Within anarchist circles there's an overall attitude of asceticism I reject. I appreciate this is a totally different world now and things are tough financially. The thing about our life was we had some money, and cost of living was so low, we didn't really have to work.

But I think deep down in the anarchist milieu there's an idea that the commodity needs to be renounced. And everything I published and believe in about the commodity is that it is human richness of a kind, but it participates in making people alienated. It's inverted. And so of course it's diseased, and of course it's destroying the planet, but that doesn't mean there isn't a profound something in there. And I think in general, my main critique of the anarchist milieu is that they reject pleasure. My entire life I've been interested in the Marquis de Sade as much Nietzsche. I think that there's an anti-political critique. There's the obvious alienation of politics and there's an anti-political critique. But I don't think the current anarchist critique goes to the level of understanding the dialectic of how the world works. I feel that the purity and the asceticism is not just cultural, but rather it's based on a lack of understanding of how richness can be used and subverted.

    I was around for the punk scene of course. I went to some of the events in San Francisco. I was aware of it. But for me ultimately it seemed like posing. I think the society said at some point that you can pose all you want, you can appear to be bad, but don't be really bad. For many people in the alternative music scene posing is now practically like breathing. The punk scene survives today as a pure appearance of resistance. And, of course, you could say the same thing about the Situationists too. They had a pretentious attitude, but they also had a critique. It's important to say that however people rebel, whatever form it takes, as long as it contains an implicit or explicit critique of work or consumption, it is helpful, it undermines this world. Unquestionably, however it happens, I'm for it.

How would you describe your politics or your political or philosophical views as they are currently?

I continue to want to play the role I took up fifty years ago. I think what we were always best at in the CEM and what I've been best at for years, how I've made a living, and how I've thought about radical tactics, is using existing media in playful ways. And that is the old category of detournement. But my thinking is a little different. For example, when people are talking about defacing or subverting the urban environment and are focusing on graffiti. I love graffiti. I don't see much now that moves me, but I was moved by graffiti in another time, and there occasionally are interesting things out there. I'm working on projects so that I can pay money to rent billboards and go that route. Because I think in a way it's not that different than publishing books. You're using traditional media. According to the current anarchist outlaw code you don't raise money. You don't do crowdsourcing to pay for billboards. It's hands-off. If it's a radical message, does it have to be presented in this street rat way? It shows in a way that you have money, you can raise money, and you have resources. You're not just a pauper dressed in black, pierced, and tattooed wandering around. The other thing is you don't have to rent that many billboards because now people will take pictures of them and go viral with them. I did the budget check. It's really not expensive. You can find a billboard in a city for $2,000 a month. That's an example of how I've been raised as a Situationist on playful surprise. I'm focused on having really socially interactive, fun experiences. And if that isn't the core of the activity, I'm not interested. That's the trend that's gone through everything I've tried to do. And, of course, I faded away and came back once or twice, but I'm still here.

What period would you say is the period where you were having the most fun? Did it happen to parallel your age? In other words, being very young?

Not very young. I had a three-year-old son and I was thirty-four when I was working on Call It Sleep. Having it be popular and playing with the medium, that really worked for me. And we talked about it before, there were so many great donations and there was so much community support, it was powerful. I think I was probably happiest in the editing room doing that project.

Can you comment on anything you may have forgotten that we would find valuable about Jean-Pierre or about his work and his project?

JP is an interesting, complex guy. The writing is cold and analytical in some ways and Hegelian, which is not my favorite school of philosophy. But as a person he's extremely different, which is not really surprising. I think the key to understanding JP is knowing what his idea of a successful revolution is. What is the world like after that happens or while it's happening? He says it's all bavardage, talking, communication, talking with consequence. He was shaped by what happened in '68 when people didn't sleep for four days because they finally had something to say to each other and couldn't talk enough because all the important questions were posed. And that's a very different idea than the Invisible Committee and all these Communist groups who say we need committees of, for example, nuclear engineers to solve our problems of decommissioning power plants. The French had this wonderful experience when they were in Paris in May 1968 and none of the problems that seemed to be problems were problems. The farmers brought food for free. They didn't even have to be asked. They showed up. They fed the entire Latin Quarter. The food was all given away without a group of leftist wankers organizing it. The real problem is how do we finally start the real conversations about the world in the right context. It just happened back then. I read some of the Invisible Committee texts. I thought . . . "You guys are idiots. You don't know what you're talking about. You have no idea what's going to happen. I don't either, but I know it's not going to be what you're talking about. Rather, it's going to be something where a humorous, intelligent, imaginative conversation solves the problems that we are told are unsolvable. They're going to happen in a couple of hours, or days, and then you're going to have to really figure out what it means to be human." That's my understanding of the process. And that's what I love about Jean-Pierre. Bavardage isn't even talking, it's chatting, which is a very intimate kind of communication, like the way we're talking to each other right now. Imagine if people on a larger scale can have this kind of conversation and ask these questions of each other.

Jean-Pierre began to formulate this idea that it was necessary for the Situationists or post-Situationists, or whatever you want to call him, to apply the same method to the critique of the SI that the Situationists had applied to the world. And the reason it was necessary is that the revolution or the radical movement that had washed up on the beach of '68 had clearly failed. Jean-Pierre's critique of the SI's theory was that Debord, in Society of the Spectacle, had assumed all of the mistakes of Marx and Marxism. It was tricky though, because they managed to confuse people in a way by using this concept of the spectacle, which, though it was certainly not an intentional smoke screen, acted as this covering abstraction. You couldn't really tell on some days, or in some reads, or in some paragraphs, that they were repeating this materialist Marxist critique. And the solution to that, obviously if you're going to get out of that trap, one has to turn to Hegel. You can't really avoid dealing with him because he had a profound critique of materialism, a kind of secular spiritualism. What Jean-Pierre brought to the party was that he said the Situationists and Debord were repeating this notion that men are animals who live to eat and eat to live, not communicators. When he showed up with that analysis, he was immediately rejected by Debord. There's a correspondence between the two of them in the early seventies about this, later joined by Gérard Lebovici. Lebovici was very important in France because he started a publishing company, Champs Libre, and let Debord pick whatever books he wanted to publish, resulting in a major

onslaught of commercially produced radical literature. There's a correspondence between Jean-Pierre and the two of them, and JP said Marx has never been criticized. We need to criticize Marx. And SI said no, we don't need to criticize Marx. They said we're right, everything is okay.

Jean-Pierre started this process in the seventies. He was going to be Debord's successor. Debord said, "You're the most brilliant guy in the milieu." I don't know if he thought he was going to die soon. It was years before he killed himself. "I want to anoint you literally as my successor," and there are conversations that took place on that topic. And then Jean-Pierre, not in order to challenge Debord, but because he was a curious philosophical mind, a critical mind, began from the perspective "If our enemies are still standing, and have taken over, and have reestablished their control, and are the ones who are really changing the world ferociously in order to stay in power, there is something wrong with the ideas that claim to attack this world."
Jean-Pierre began this process, and we have some forthcoming literature we're publishing (An Inquiry into the Causes and Nature of the Misery of People) that shows that by 1978 he had formulated this critique and he was immediately ostracized. They said he was a little crazy but mostly he was just wrong. The Debordists said that there was no reason to make a critique of Marx and the Situationists. Why would anyone say there's no reason to make a critique of anything if it's a good critique? But this was the wet blanket tactic. Voyer had been published by Debord's publishing house, Champs Libre, himself. He had been involved in selling their books all over France. There were many times when Debord as the pope of the movement had kicked people out who probably deserved to be kicked out. And this is maybe one of the few times that he actually excluded somebody, although he wasn't part of the group because the group had been dissolved, who didn't deserve it. Jean-Pierre found his

own way. I think the reason that Tikkun or the Pro-Situs haven't done a critique of Marx and the Situationists is that it is really hard to do. They would always make a few minor comments, but it was all about style never about substance. He was alone in this. It's hard to figure out an intelligent way to say that Marx was half-right and the Situationists were half-right, to keep everything that's good and suppress what isn't. That's the art—to never throw out the baby with the bathwater. To remember everything and acknowledge everything that they did positively and negatively. I think Jean-Pierre did a good job. He loved them passionately and yet he saw that if we didn't turn the negative scalpel on them it would make revolt more difficult. It's not like the world can't change without a critique of the Situationists, it's just that their ideas are very influential. I really believe that. I like that slogan, "The last cops are in our heads." I feel that's a very powerful thing to say, and it's easy to forget in the current era, and that's why Reich: How to Use (text by Jean-Pierre) is an important text to remember.

That's the legacy that I'm trying to help carry forward from that period, not from the Situationists but from Jean-Pierre, is to actually take that analytic process and look at the people who seem to be closest to you with that subversive eye. It's highly discouraged now, in this climate we live in now.

In this case though, these ideas that Jean-Pierre criticized from Marx, they're really among the most influential ideas in the world. The bourgeoisie, the technocrats, our rulers, the oligarchs, they've all read Marx. They have all understood him to a certain extent, they've all appropriated Marx. When you're making a critique of Marx, and in some ways the SI because they've appropriated him, the key is to stay away from personalities as much as possible. JP ultimately took on Debord because he was such a hero. But not others. He didn't do a character assassination of the entire SI at the time. It was one man who stood for the most radical critique of the modern world. He and his life and his personality became synonymous with that. I think it was okay in a way for him to go there to pull the rug out from under the whole thing.

Do you find that anarchist organization was a little bit pregnant with Bolshevism back in the sixties or today? And what would you summarize as the main difference that sets apart Situationist groups from Bay Area anarchist groups?

The French Situationists definitely had a solid hierarchical structure, given that Guy Debord played the role of pope and his writings were treated as the holy sacrament. But our version of the rules of the game in America when we first started was not like the Situationists. We did not have a Debord. We had no great theories and, in the end, we were not theorists really. We were all actors, subversives. We were all juvenile delinquents because we were basically still in a juvenile delinquent age. We were twenty-one. People forget we were forced to be really mature in certain ways, by the era, once we accepted the responsibilities of the critics of leftism. But we were just kids. We were fuckups. It wasn't like the Weather Underground story, where everyone was spoiled and rich. Some people in our group were dirt poor. One of them, Bill Davis, literally grew up almost like a sharecropper in Sacramento, and he was drawn to the ideas too. We were definitely different from the anarchists. They were all about this constant regurgitation of the Spanish anarchist history. I think we were pretty much anti-ideological. We borrowed from William Burroughs, and from the surrealists. We were very eclectic and we were constantly insulting the crap out of all the Bolsheviks, including the Black Panthers. We said, "These people are ideologues, fuck them all."

What's your opinion of the work of Debord and Vaneigem?

Alternatingly over my life I've gone in and out of love with both of them many times for various reasons. That's not an easy question. I was reading about this slogan, "Ne Travailez Jamais," ("Never Work") because I wanted to do a fifiteth anniversary event for May '68. It turned out the first person to make this slogan public that we know of was Guy Debord, in 1953. How can you knock that? How can you knock this young kid who writes that on a wall in Paris? Brilliant, right? It meant "never fucking work as human beings." I was influenced heavily by both of them. I would have to say now, given how I've described my attitude towards playfulness, that in the end I think I'm more influenced by Vaneigem.

www.ingramcontent.com/pod-product-compliance
Lightning Source LLC
Chambersburg PA
CBRC090746010526
44114CB00008B/97